Michael Aleksiuk and Thomas Nelson, Editors

Landscapes of the Heart

NARRATIVES OF NATURE AND SELF

NEWEST PRESS

National Library of Canada Cataloguing in Publication Data
Main entry under title:

Landscapes of the heart

1. Landscape--Psychological aspects. 2. Nature (Aesthetics) I. Aleksiuk, Michael, 1942- II. Nelson, T. M. (Thomas Morgan), 1924-
BH301.L3L36 2002 111'.85 C2002-910044-5

Editor for the Press: Don Kerr
Cover photography: www.comstock.com (front top), Michael Aleksiuk (front bottom and backcover)
Cover and book design: Ruth Linka

The Canada Council for the Arts since 1957 | Le Conseil des Arts du Canada depuis 1957

Canadian Heritage Patrimoine canadien

NeWest Press acknowledges the support of the Canada Council for the Arts and The Alberta Foundation for the Arts for our publishing program. We also acknowledge the financial support of the Government of Canada through the Book Publishing Industry Development Program (BPIDP) for our publishing activities.

NeWest Press
201-8540-109 Street
Edmonton, Alberta
T6G 1E6
(780) 432-9427
www.newestpress.com

1 2 3 4 5 04 03 02 01 02

PRINTED AND BOUND IN CANADA

THIS BOOK IS PRINTED ON ANCIENT FOREST-FRIENDLY PAPER

Landscapes of the Heart

This book is dedicated to everyone who
has experienced the emotional and spiritual
benefits of natural environments, even
if only during a quiet walk in a city park.

"I live not in myself, but I become
Portion of that around me; and to me
High Mountains are a feeling . . ."

Lord Byron

Contents

Preface

AS MEMBERS OF AN URBANIZED WESTERN CIVILIZATION, WE are all too often totally dislocated from natural aspects of the world. There aren't many of us today who don't feel something natural is missing from our lives. A person may have sufficient food, shelter, clothing, cars and more than enough acquaintances to share those essentials with, yet the absence of nature can create an emptiness, a feeling something isn't quite right. Hence the enormous, ever-increasing appeal of national parks, wilderness areas, lakeside campgrounds, public gardens and city parks. To what degree does the growing popularity of gardening reflect our need for contact with living nature?

Most of us experience a sense of place in the natural landscape, in one form or another. We've experienced a moment when a natural place "felt right," even if only fleetingly. Frequently we treasure our relationship to a specific place in nature, and nurture it with care. Each in his own way, both Thomas Nelson and I have such relationships to special natural places. During the early stages of the conceptualization of this book, we held two-hour sessions weekly for almost an entire year, discussing this subject rigorously. We focused on the developing fields of environmental psychology and ecopsychology, not so much from an academic perspective but rather as those two fields relate to the emotional needs of people in the community at large. Nelson and I went on trips into the hills and boreal forests of northern Alberta. I have never seen Nelson more relaxed than on one trip, when we walked through a large expanse of old growth boreal forest north of Wandering River. He closely examined some small balsam firs, almost lovingly. I watched with pleasure as Nelson moved through the forested landscape. Nelson became part of the landscape, every bit at home as a bear or a wolf.

Over a period of one year Nelson and I got to know each other's deepest feelings concerning the emotional and therapeutic dimensions of walks through old growth forests, and indeed through any natural area. When it comes to emotional/therapeutic/spiritual benefits of natural environments, it is feelings more than thoughts that count. I became acutely aware of just how important a personal relationship to a natural place can be, and assumed other people must share this value for natural places. So, I created a website on the subject and emailed individuals at universities, inviting them to submit chapters for consideration in an anthology on the subject of personal relationships to the natural world. I asked people to explore their own experiences with nature, especially as those experiences relate to their personal well-being.

The response was overwhelming. People clearly resonated to the concept of a special natural place in their lives, a place they either currently cherished or sorely missed. More than two hundred chapter proposals were received in the editorial offices, of which one hundred were eventually delivered to me as complete manuscripts. Fifty-five chapters merited serious consideration, and some thirty-five were judged to be of major interest to like-minded readers. In consultation with press editor Don Kerr of NeWest Press, I selected a sample of eleven for inclusion in this book. I hope you enjoy reading these essays as much as I enjoyed putting them together.

The title of this book, *Landscapes of the Heart*, was taken from the essay by Douglas Porteous.

Michael Aleksiuk
Edmonton, Canada

Foreword

Maurice Strong
CHAIR, EARTH COUNCIL

AS WE MOVE INTO THE 21ST CENTURY, HUMAN INGENUITY and the miracles wrought by our accomplishments in science and technology have produced a civilization beyond the wildest dreams of earlier generations and given us the tools with which to shape an even more exciting and promising future. But these same forces have also given rise to some serious and deepening imbalances which must be seen as ominous threats to our common future. The gap between rich and poor, privileged and underprivileged, is deepening, both within and amongst societies, and is an affront to the moral basis of our civilization. This process, if it is not reversed, will inevitably lead to greater social tensions and potential for conflict in the new millennium. The personal reflections in this book are important examples of how we need to reconnect with ourselves and our environment if we are to overcome these obstacles and achieve a sustainable society for all in the new millennium.

In 1992, world leaders gathering at the Earth Summit in Rio de Janeiro agreed that achieving sustainable development requires a fundamental change in the dynamics and direction of our economic life. They agreed to assert a new political and moral will which would in turn produce the social and economic innovation required to devise the means to deal effectively with both present and future imbalances.

In the years since the Earth Summit, many political leaders have disappointed us by failing to integrate basic changes to which they agreed at Rio into the policies and laws which would put our societies on the path to sustainability. Disillusionment with our political system has led us to look toward ourselves and our "civil society" institutions to lead the necessary changes.

Though we cannot let our political leaders off the hook, we as individuals must take the initiative to commit ourselves to our own personal moral, ethical, and spiritual renaissance, and then and only then will the priorities of society respond to the values of people. Indeed, we are already witnessing an historic convergence between the practical aspects of human life and its moral and spiritual dimensions in efforts such as the global campaign to develop a Peoples Earth Charter. It is hoped that the Earth Charter will function as a universal ethical code of conduct which will guide persons and nations with respect to sustainable development and ecological security. The deeply personal explorations of self and environment in this book are testimony that this is occurring.

I commend the contributors to this book as they have bridged the dichotomy between the "real world" of practical affairs and the more ethereal, ideal world of morals and spirit as we strive towards a sustainable future for humankind and this planet. Their work collectively embodies what I believe to be the only way that we can move forward as a global society: by recognizing that achieving sustainable development is not only about policies and law-making; it is also a moral and spiritual journey upon which the foundations for a sustainable way of life on our planet will be built.

The River

Lisa Lynch

IT WAS EARLY SATURDAY AFTERNOON OF 3 MAY 1975. THE RIVER behind our house was high and fast, rushing down the flanks of the western Cascade mountains in Oregon. All morning Dad had been out fishing, running our red riverboat up and down the swift current. It was a good boat. He had modified it by putting a steering column in the middle so we wouldn't have to twist our backs using the outboard motor. The boat was made of wood; the inside was painted white. Sometimes he would let me take it out alone. The boat would glide up the current effortlessly. Being only fourteen, I would listen to the latest popular songs play in my head—enjoying the speed, the wind, and the river.

Dad asked Robin (my eleven-year-old sister) and me if we wanted to go for a boat ride. Robin was playing Barbies on the living room floor with her friend Shelly, who wanted to go along too. We all piled into the boat, my dad started the engine, and we headed upstream.

We followed the bend and made our way toward Amacher Park. This time of year we didn't normally go up over the rapids just before the park. But Dad had been doing it all day so he figured we could go up this time too. We nosed into the rapids—they were full and exciting, the whitewater cresting in high roaring waves. We bounced up through the riffles and into the first big wave. Then the motor, for some reason, faltered. The nose of the boat went directly into the wave. The boat filled with water, turned broadside, and capsized. We were all thrown into the current. The water was so cold. I remember Dad yelling. I can still hear the panic in his voice. Robin grabbed onto me, pulling me under. I struggled and pushed her away. All four of us came up next to the boat, which was completely submerged. It looked like a white cloud under the water. The bank of the river wasn't far away, but the current was strong. There were no houses on the nearest shore, so I started to swim for the opposite side. I could hear Robin screaming. The current was taking her away.

"Grab onto the bushes!" I yelled at her. "Pull yourself out! I'm going for help!"

I saw her go under.

The submerged willows dragged across my legs as I struggled toward shore. I could see Dad's head, and Shelly clinging to him. I was the first one out. I ran to our neighbor's house.

"There's been an accident!" I yelled.

They didn't find Robin that night. My best friend Cindi came over to be with me and to help in the house. Many people were coming and going, crying and looking scared. The nightly news announced to the community the tragedy of the accident. As of news time they said her body still hadn't been found. The river was unpredictable; she could be anywhere. Some believed she could still be alive. I just kept seeing her being pulled under by the river, carried down the fast, determined stream, and I could still feel the cold helplessness in my own body, dragging across the submerged willows, as I swam away from her to the opposite shore

I crawled further and further inside myself as the divers continued to look. They looked, my father looked. We continued in that terrible suspended place for twenty-three days. They made some sort of an announcement on the evening news every night. Then one day I was in the bathroom brushing my teeth and I heard a car coming down our gravel driveway. I looked out the window—it was a sheriff's car. I knew. They had found her body.

Looking for His Daughter's Body

Each day after the accident
he would move up and down the
current of the river in a gold,
swift, flat-bottomed fishing boat

looking for his daughter's body.

Up and down the current, what
were the images driving him?
For 20 days he looked

while his wife curled up on
the gold crushed-velvet couch
in disbelief and terrible pain.

Neighbors helped look
and brought chocolate cake.
Because they heard I liked it.

Then it changed to angel food
because the story of what I
liked had changed.

We waited like that,
stunned. News reports
invaded mother's soft heart
each day until she asked
"Sweetheart, let them find you."

And the divers did, that day.

I watched him from the
back of a soft gray horse,
listening to the sucking sounds
of hooves walking along
the river bank

looking for her body
waiting until they found her

exactly where I had known she
was all along.

He sold the boat then
and joined mother on the gold couch.

LISA LYNCH

The funeral came and went, children
sang and school bus 49 sent flowers.

When it was over we tried carefully
to move towards each other
but our pain was too great.

He looks in my eyes now
for his daughter's body.
Because my eyes, for 18 years
still move up and down
the river continuous and
faithful in their looking.

River Days

Six years before the accident, in 1969, my father sold his partnership in a hydraulic cylinder manufacturing plant in Los Angeles, moved his family to a southern Oregon logging town, and re-opened his business. My parents didn't want to raise their two children in an area of violence, where drug deals took place in elementary school yards. So we tranquilized our gray cat, packed ourselves into our black and white '68 Cadillac, and headed north. My younger sister and I were elated. When my parents first told me that we were moving to Oregon, the first thing I asked was, "Can I have a horse?" I loved the outdoors, and moved to our rental house on five acres of forest and fenced pastures with the boundless energy of a nine-year-old. I became the cowgirl of my early childhood dreams, roaming the hills and pastures that surrounded our house.

A year later we moved into another house, on an acre of land along the North Umpqua River. I'll never forget the first time I saw what we came to call "the river house." The outside was painted bright lime green with pale green inner walls and horrible green (of course!) carpeting. There was a large white-fenced corral in the front, being used at the time as a flower garden. It became a place for my second horse, a gray gelding named Smoky who delighted in stomping the flowers and became colicky from eating too many apples from the overhanging apple trees. The backyard of the house was almost an acre of lawn ending at the bank of the river. I remember standing in the backyard looking out at the river the day we moved into the house. Its rushing water called out to me, meeting the surging wildness of my young soul.

We spent the summer days swimming in the river's pools behind the house. Large black truck-tire inner tubes dotted the lawns. We would roll the tubes, inflated to full capacity and cracking under the hot sun, down the hill and watch them splash into the river. Then we would climb onto them and float slowly downstream, heading to River Forks Park six miles away. About halfway to the park there was a formidable set of rapids called Burkhardt. It was always a rite of passage to make it through. On one of our first trips down the river, when I was about eleven years old, my inner tube began losing air before we made it to the park. My grandfather graciously traded his inner tube for mine. I ended up going over Burkhardt Rapids for the first time that day. My sister Robin, at eight years old, was still too young to go over, so my grandfather took her out of the river and walked her around the rapids. I remember watching the two of them as they found their way carefully, hand in hand, along the rocks of the river bank. I remember the sunlight flashing in Robin's hair and the shouts of floaters sliding down the falls, submerging and popping up in the final roll of the rapids.

The next summer Robin made her first trip through Burkhardt Rapids. I was with her and I remember we screamed the whole way through.

I loved fishing in the river. Robin and I would run down to the water's edge in the morning and catch rainbow trout for breakfast. Fishing poles lined the back of our house—slim fly rods, small trout poles, and the heavier salmon rods. Fishing was part of our day, like reading the morning paper, feeding the horses, or getting the mail. We took it for granted. We would sit in the sun on the riverbank and tell stories about how in the "olden days" you used to be able to walk across the river on the backs of migrating salmon. Salmon and trout were part of our lives. Neighbors would swap fishing stories and friends would argue over whose catch was the biggest.

One summer day—it must've been in the afternoon because I remember the warmth of the sun on my back, illuminating the cottonwoods across the river—I was fishing for trout with my fancy brown trout rod, casting above a rock shelf I had been swimming over earlier in the day. I was using a flashy fishing lure, being too lazy to bait the hook or maybe not wanting to deal with the mess. Just cast and drift, reel in, cast and drift. All the time I was wandering slowly downstream toward the rapids.

Suddenly a fish hit my lure. I set the hook, thinking it was a trout.

The line pulled taut and I thought I had snagged the bottom. Then it jerked in a way that told me I had a very large fish on. Alone, without a net, I was fighting a mighty steelhead of the North Umpqua on my small trout rod. I had light test line—sure to break. I moved with the fish up and down the current, shaking with excitement, already forming the story in my mind, picturing the celebration of my family when I walked up the hill with a wild steelhead! My father would brag, my friends would all be jealous, and Mom would certainly get out the camera! The fish kept fighting . . . and fighting.

Finally I landed it in a small pool above the rapids. The steelhead was at least eight pounds, and a beautiful catch. I hooked my fingers through its gills and hung on. The fish gave one last flip and I had it on the rocks. Without a net, on a trout rod!

I had a secret though. We all did. It wasn't really the fish we were after; it was the river. Being close to the river, we got to learn its moods and currents—where the snags were, how the fishing line would play over a certain submerged rock ledge, where the lure could safely sink in front of the imagined fish. Fishing became a kind of meditation. When a fish bit or tugged at a line, the adrenalin rush became the communion. That is what we waited for: the tug, the movement from under the dark water that said to us, "I am alive, and I know you are there."

In the fall, around Thanksgiving, the river would almost always rise. The rains could fill the river within hours. I would stand at the end of our lawn in my rubber hip waders and watch the brown water rise up over my toes to my ankles and knees, and then I'd step back and watch it come closer and closer to me. The river turned into a brown, rolling giant, much different from the beautiful blue-green of summer.

The rise of the river in the fall was always a time of unspoken celebration. Robin and I would be let out of school early lest the water cross the road and block our school buses. At home we were excited to see how high the river had come since morning. I would put on my hip-boots and rain jacket and take a twenty-foot-long aluminum pole down to meet the rising water. Because of extensive clear-cutting upstream, tons of woody debris left behind by the loggers would be washed by landslides and flooding creeks into the river. I would spend the whole day and into the evening pushing the debris off our lawn and back into the current. If we missed a log, in a matter of minutes we might have a log jam. That would bring out the fathers in the neighborhood, who would wade into the floodwater with chainsaws and cut away the debris. If they didn't, a mass of logs and tangled branches would cause a dangerous backwash. We listened to the radio constantly, waiting for the announcement of when the river would crest and at what flood stage. It was an exciting time.

When the river crested—meaning the water would stop rising, pause like a slack tide, and begin to recede—it became even more important to push the debris off the lawn. If we failed to do so, it would be late spring before we got around to cleaning the logs and other debris from the lawn. But if we worked while the river was cresting, we could tend the receding water-line with our poles and pitch forks, tossing back the logging debris or the tangled wood blown down during wind storms.

Once a school friend came over to help with the flood. She went into the river with her hipwaders on and turned her back upstream. "Never turn your back to a flooding river!" I yelled at her, "A log could come along and knock your feet right out from under you. Never, never turn your back on the river."

I was twelve years old, and already wise to the ways of the river.

Grief and Healing

For months after Robin drowned I could barely look at the river. I tended my horses and went back to school, moving as if underwater, a weight constant and un-nameable holding down the life in my own body. Mom and Dad continued with their lives as best they could. I remember the first time I set the dinner table for just three instead of four. It seemed awkward, impossible, wrong. But we were carried through our days by some invisible force—love and caring from neighbors, family, the church, and each other. I felt angry at the river, something that was hard for me because of my intense relationship with it.

School ended and the weather began to warm. Normally we would be planning our first float and starting to swim in the still-too-cold river. I remember standing up by the house just staring down at the bank, staring with such a new feeling for the river in my chest I could hardly describe it. I hated the river, but I was irretrievably wound into it too. Something about Robin's death had brought the river closer to me, in a fierce way.

I finally entered the river a few months later. I was alone. The water against my skin felt cold and strong. I stood there for a long time, because it was cold and because I was afraid. My fear wasn't about diving in; it was different. I was facing a force that I had never known before. The river was suddenly awesome and powerful, and I wasn't sure how to respond. I dove in. The water was murky, but I opened my eyes and saw the bottom. I saw Robin's face and her white tennis shoe bobbing up and down in the current—that's how the divers found her body. When I came up for air there was a different feeling between me and the river. Somehow I'd managed to dive in, despite my fear, back into a body that I had once loved, a body that had formed my spirit. At that moment I realized my relationship with the river was too important for me to turn away. By diving in, I had made a wild gesture that at age fourteen I could only embody and not name.

Recently I told Mom and Dad about my first dive into the river after the accident. "What do you think that must have been like for your mother and I?" Dad asked. Suddenly a part of the story I hadn't acknowledged unfolded before me. I had focused on my own pain, my heroic gesture of diving back in, when up in the house behind partially opened curtains Mom and Dad must have felt a primal fear that they had to hold back out of respect for my relationship with the river.

Dad told me that for about a year both he and Mom could not look at the river. They kept the drapes drawn over all the windows that faced it. Then one day, for whatever reason, the curtains were opened; that was their dive back in a gesture that said to the river, "I see you, but I see you with torn-open eyes."

My parents remodeled the house, painted it, and changed the front yard. Robin's bedroom was remodeled into a large master bedroom with its own bathroom and Jacuzzi tub. The garage was modeled into a family room with dark carpet and paneling. Robin's piano was traded for a player piano with rolls and rolls of preprinted songs—"Hello Dolly," "When the Saints Come Marching In," "Silent Night," and many others played over and over and over again. I moved my horses up the hill onto the old turkey farm and we turned the pasture into a vegetable garden. Slowly the house and the land began to change into a new form, and we opened the drapes every morning. I swam in the river as much as ever, floating and bodysurfing the rapids.

On 7 July 1984 I was married in the backyard of the river house. The night before the wedding, drunk from the wine and champagne at the rehearsal dinner, our best man Todd, my maid of honor Cindi, my husband-to-be Kevin and I went skinny-dipping in the warm, starlit water of the river. We rolled in the dark water like otters. The evening became a celebration of all that the river had given me over the years. The next afternoon in the gazebo, next to the rose garden behind the house, Kevin read Shakespeare and I cried from nervous joy while trying to say our wedding vows. After the ceremony our next-door-neighbor Dick came up the river to our backyard in his blue sled boat covered with flowers and with a large, handwritten sign stretched along the boat's side saying "Just Married." I threw my bouquet into the crowd and Kevin and I jumped into the boat and went up the river spraying champagne, laughing, and waving to the surprised crowd. We went gliding up the river together, to Amacher Park, over the rapids that just nine years before had swamped our red fishing boat. I thought of Robin that day, but the laughter and the numbness from the alcohol moving through my veins kept those painful memories at bay. I held my new husband's hand as we went through the rapids and waved to Cindi and Todd, who had driven ahead to meet us at the park.

Sometimes, even today, when I dive into the river and open my eyes I still see the white tennis shoe bobbing in the murky current. I can still see her small lifeless body held by the submerged willows, silently waiting to be found.

The River's Story

I returned to the North Umpqua River in 1993 to work on my master's thesis in ecopsychology: a comprehensive study of the geology, natural history, human history, and current ecological concerns surrounding the river—all interwoven with my personal story of growing up on the river. I was drawn by the complexity of the environmental issues surrounding the river, as well as by my own love and respect for it.

As I studied the history of the North Umpqua I learned of the pioneer settlers' tremendous impact on the land as they traveled across the country: the murder of Aboriginal people, the extraction of tons of salmon and steelhead, the harvesting of millions of board feet of timber, the greed of the bounty hunters, and the disturbance of native ecology by the settlers, their cultivation of domestic plants and raising of livestock. How could I tell this sad story? I gathered facts in the same way I used to pick the green beans grown in the river valley: carefully, methodically, thoroughly. And it left my body stiff with pain.

I then turned to the current environmental controversies swirling around the river. The diminishing salmon and trout populations, warming tributaries, and gaping clear-cuts all formed a chorus of grief that I suddenly shared.

Salmon

When I went back to the river in 1993 to swim in my old swimming hole behind our house, I dove in and was shocked at the warmth of the water. Usually there was a breath-catching chill to the fast current—but on this day in mid-summer the water seemed warmer than I had remembered it. I was startled and concerned. The river was different; it felt like some of the wildness was gone. I later found out the temperature at Winchester Dam, not far from our house, had reached eighty degrees Fahrenheit.

In talking with the local Oregon Department of Fish and Wildlife staff, I discovered that the increased temperature of the water was due to extensive clear-cutting along the streams that are tributaries of the river. Without the trees and surrounding vegetation to shade the streams, the exposed water is warmed and runs into the river. When this happens to several of the river's tributaries, the overall temperature of the river is increased.

One summer afternoon in 1997 I was flying with my dad in his small plane over the Umpqua National Forest on a sightseeing trip to

Crater Lake. Observing the forest from a small plane was agonizing. The patchwork of clear-cuts stretched across the land like a tattered quilt. The only continuous forest I could see was a small patch of wilderness known as Boulder Creek. My heart was breaking—tears rose in my eyes as we flew over the river canyon. Entire drainages were clear-cut—ragged areas of "experimental harvesting" and complete clear-cuts were linked together along the river corridor. My dad said quietly, "There are still some trees left."

"Not many," I replied. "Not many." My body was cringing from the memory of diving into the too-warm water of the river several years before.

One of the most notable impacts of the warm water is the effect it has on the runs of migrating salmon and trout that have graced the North Umpqua since the last ice age. I was astonished and alarmed when I discovered the salmon and steelhead counts had kept dropping from 10,576 fish in 1990 to 4,873 fish in 1991 (resulting in the first emergency fishing closure on the North Umpqua River) and down to 3,776 in 1992. I knew intuitively that some kind of threshold had been crossed. I wondered if the salmon could ever come back.

One afternoon while doing my research, sitting in the office of the US Forest Service, a fax came in from the Department of Natural Resources. It was a press release announcing a petition recommending that there be an emergency listing of the North Umpqua searun cutthroat trout as an endangered species. As of that date—19 August 1993—no searun cutthroat had returned to spawn in the North

Umpqua. Amid quite a stir in the office, I photocopied the fax. As I sat there reading it, realizing that as of that date no trout had been counted in the river, I wondered if endangered was the right listing and what extinct meant! I spoke with biologists and fishermen, trying to understand the nature of the problem, and to find out what the plan was to restore the trout and reverse the plummeting population counts.

The North Umpqua cutthroat trout was finally listed as an endangered species on 9 August 1996. It took almost three years of studies, meetings, and lawsuits before the National Marine Fisheries Service (NMFS) could agree to this action. This was the first such listing in the State of Oregon for an anadromous (migrating) fish. The local agencies and fishing organizations assumed that this listing would eliminate the release of any timber sales that would further compromise or damage the habitat of the cutthroat trout. Instead, it was determined by the NMFS that the restrictions placed by the Northwest Forest Plan were enough to protect the habitat of the trout. So, under the protection of the timber salvage rider passed by the Clinton administration, sixty-three timber sales were released in the North Umpqua watershed—sales that had previously been determined by the Environmental Protection Agency to be degrading cutthroat trout habitat. This prompted a lawsuit, filed on 7 May 1997, by local environmental and fishing groups to counteract the release of any additional timber sales.

Toketee

During the conquest to harness the potential energy from the rivers of the west, the North Umpqua was not overlooked. The Toketee Project on the upper North Umpqua is a forty-four-mile system of eight dams, reservoirs, and conduits. The Chinook word *toketee* means beautiful or graceful. What I discovered was something quite different. "A River at Work for Growth and Progress" was the title of the report I got from the Oregon Department of Fish and Wildlife. According to the report, the original reconnaissance of the North Umpqua to determine possible hydroelectric project sites in the region was done in 1922. The report, generated by the California Oregon Power Company (COPCO), recommended construction of two dams: a 220-foot dam at Rock Creek and a 187-foot dam at the boundary of the National Forest. The construction of these two dams would have flooded the entire upper reaches of the North Umpqua, forever filling vast canyons of old-growth forest and towering basalt monoliths, as well as destroying what turned out to be a very profitable fishery (two million dollars annually). Fortunately the dams were voted down by the Hydroelectric Commission because of the interference with the building of roads which were to connect eastern and western Oregon.

Twenty-three years later COPCO returned with an application to the Federal Energy Regulatory Commission (FERC) for another license to build the Toketee Project—seven hydroelectric plants constructed in the upper reaches of the North Umpqua that would not interfere with road development. In 1947 licenses were issued and construction continued until 1956, essentially closing the river to any fishing because of unnatural and dangerous fluctuations of the river due to the construction. According to Frank Moore, who owned the fishing lodge Steamboat Inn at the time, "When the construction began on the Toketee Power Project, the river fluctuated wildly and filled with silt. This destroyed salmon redds [nests] and made the fishing unsafe. Just before the fishing season began in the summer of 1952, with my reservation books filled, the river became unsafe for fishing. We had to close the Steamboat Inn from 1952 to 1955. Since then, the river has never been the same."

I didn't know about this dam system when I was growing up on the river. There was a small hydroelectric plant at Winchester, near our house, but I thought I was living on a wild, untamed river. In 1988 a section of the river had even been designated a Wild and Scenic Waterway by the federal government. When I discovered the extent of the past hydroelectric construction, I was shocked. I learned that a "lake" I had played and fished in as a child is actually a reservoir that is drained in the winter for power needs. I was struck by the irony of the lake's Chinook name "Lemolo," which means wild or untamed.

At the time of my research, COPCO had to re-license the project (its existing license expired in 1995). And I found out they were applying to do further construction. (As of 1998 they still hadn't been granted a license.) Already water from the river was being hauled up miles and miles of canals and flumes. What COPCO also proposed, in addition to existing construction, was to harness the energy from some of the tributaries, for example one area called Watson Falls. I had visited Watson Falls many times, and it was an especially memorable part of my honeymoon along the river. I was told that COPCO was proposing to "redirect" the falls into a canal and flume system. In response to an uproar by the local community, COPCO retracted its application and proposed that the water be redirected only during the evening hours. I couldn't believe it—they were going to turn one of the most beautiful natural sites along the river into a faucet! I was recently assured that this part of the application was denied.

During the summer of 1993 a friend sent me a newspaper clipping about a conference in nearby Springfield, Oregon called "Instream Flows for Recreation." Sponsored by the National Park Service and Oregon State University, the conference featured a guided white-water trip down the North Umpqua River. I couldn't miss it! I called the director of the conference and explained what I was working on, asking if there was a reduced fee for students or perhaps a work-study position I could fill. He said he would get back to me. He didn't. So—I just showed up at the Double Tree Inn and found him. I explained to him that I really needed to just sit in on a few talks to get a general idea of what the conference would be covering. He never really said yes; he just handed me the materials and walked away.

I noticed in one of the illustrated descriptions that they actually called the river a faucet! I couldn't believe it—I felt like I was in the enemy camp. They spoke about how to design surveys that measured a floater's, kayaker's or rafter's preference for a particular flow of water down the stream. The flow of the river would be adjusted using the spillways from the dams. Then a group would float or kayak down the river. Each time, the users would fill out a questionnaire about what they liked or didn't like about a particular flow level. There were even suggestions to use dynamite to blast boulders in rapids that are unpassable and to use inflatable "rocks" to increase the quality of the experience of the "user." According to this plan, a user could enjoy floating down several different rivers in a single day! To me this seemed like they were turning the river into a roller-coaster amusement ride. And each time the river's flows were changed unnaturally, beds of salmon eggs could be exposed and fish could potentially be stranded. The people at the conference defined these issues as "conflicts of interest." What they were talking about—satisfying the human need for recreation without respect for the river's wildness—I found appalling. Shaking, and with a tight stomach, I left at the first break.

As I was finishing this work, I had a dream. I dreamt I was being lifted up over the land and asked to look back down. I saw the blue lines of watersheds up and down the western coast of North America. I realized that the story I had told of the North Umpqua was true in some form for all the small, blue, vein-like lines I was being shown. I heard the cry of the rivers, of the native people, and of the salmon. It was from within this feeling of grief, from my study of a time long ago, that I was able to enter my personal story from the river.

Letting Go

Early in the summer of 1993, during my research, I went back to the bank of the river next to the rapids where Robin drowned. I looked into the flash of the familiar swirls of water, and out across the rocks and shrubs shaping the river. Because I had come to know the river and its history so intimately, I was afforded a new relationship with it and felt I could see more clearly the nature of the river and the details of the accident. Even though I had been back to the rapids several times since the accident, they now looked different to me. I felt a sense of benevolence from the river. The water became vibrant and clear and I felt an opening in my chest, a darkness poured out and was filled with a gentle feeling. I knew I had been blessed by the river and that I could now reclaim the fourteen-year-old who crouched deep within my psyche, still looking for the body of her sister.

I could see that part of my awareness had been stuck there like an eternal repeating loop of a computer program. Over and over in my mind I pushed my sister away. For me, her body was still in the river. I had to allow the rest of the scene to play out: to see myself yelling to her to grab onto the bushes, hear her voice crying out in panic, remember the decision I'd made to swim to the shore and not go after her, remember the hope, the searching, the fear, the pain, the prayers.

Finally, I could see that the river no longer held her body, and that her drowning was not my fault. I went to the quiet cemetery and laid three purple roses on her grave under a large oak tree.

That day at her grave I heard a deep cry all around me. It was the cry of the diminishing salmon stocks, of the dammed and controlled wildness of the river, of the native people who had lived on the river for thousands of years. It was the cry of my family over the death of my sister Robin. I realized there will always be something of Robin in the river, but it isn't her body. It is her beautiful spirit, inseparable from the molecules of water that flow within the river's banks. Her constant presence touches the part of my own spirit that lives in the curves of the river's current.

Emma

I finished my master's thesis in its written form just before the spring equinox of 1994, received my master's degree soon thereafter, and took a short break in the hot springs at Brietenbush, Oregon. While I was there I felt a dissolution of an old, dark congestion in my body. I soaked in the hot springs, took long saunas, walked in the old-growth and exhaled a long breath, releasing the nineteen years of grief I had held in the contours of my heart. I met a young girl there named Emily. For some reason, she thought I was a wizard and followed me all over the camp on her little pink bicycle. I thought to myself, what a lovely name for a young girl, Emily! I went home and found a quiet place to continue my resting. A month later I was feeling ill in my dance class. I checked the calendar . . . I was pregnant!

My husband and I had been trying to get pregnant for five years and had succeeded only in creating an ectopic pregnancy that resulted in surgery and the loss of my right fallopian tube. What had been blocked had apparently been released. I went to the doctor and he assured me that I was indeed pregnant. Because of my history, he told me, we would have to do an ultrasound to locate the embryo as soon as it was visible. They took blood to determine whether my hormone level indicated that the fetus was far enough along. The next day the nurse called. "You need to have your ultrasound done right now," she said. "How long will it take you to get here?" I rushed to the clinic.

As soon as the technician placed the ultrasound on my belly, she said, "It's in your uterus!" I grabbed her white lab coat and just started crying. There was a small spot of light in the center of my dark uterus. I asked her what the blinking was. "It's the heartbeat," she said.

Seven and a half months later I gave birth to my daughter Emma. She is a bright, beautiful child and an immense blessing to our family. Not long after I gave birth to her, a feeling rose up in me that I hadn't had before—a new empathy with my own mother at the loss of her child. As a mother myself, only now could I begin to imagine what my mother's pain must've been and still is.

Exploring the river in this way was a huge challenge and a continuous struggle. As I write these words, my daughter's body climbs onto mine and I understand that we all touch each other through the unfolding of our collective stories. Now, in my dreams I see these images: the wild river bursting forth from the tangled harness of the hydroelectric project; my sister's bright smile flashing on a hot summer's day; the spirit of the river dancing in the sun-warmed clouds above a land where all hearts share a concern for all beings wild.

The Mission Mountains

Mark Schaller

AS AN UNDERGRADUATE I ONCE TOOK A RELIGION COURSE, BUT I don't recall that we studied much religion. Mostly we read contemporary novels about dreamy Americans feeling alienated from the world and the people around them. They connected only occasionally and briefly—when their cars went spinning off the highway, when falling objects shattered to the ground at their feet, or when they experienced some other sort of unpredictable brush with physical fragility.

I have two vivid memories from that class. First, I recall the time a wasp got into the classroom. The students watched that wasp for several nervous minutes as it buzzed around the windows and the lights above our heads. But the professor didn't seem to notice. He was a passionate speaker, and kept on discussing whatever he was lecturing about (that part I don't recall). At one point the wasp actually landed on his head, but he still ignored it. The rest of us watched in amazement as the wasp crawled down behind his ear and then turned on his neck and crept forward across his cheek. Finally, alerted perhaps by our gasps and gestures as the wasp crested the bridge of his nose, he started, shook the wasp aside, and went on.

The other thing I remember was a question the professor asked us one day: When are you most yourself—when you are alone, or when you are with other people?

26 *Leaving*

A couple of years ago, in the middle of July, I packed my backpack with my tent, stove, sleeping bag, two pairs of shorts and four pairs of socks, and enough food to last a week and a half. I laced up my boots, picked up my pack, and left my house. I didn't realize it at the time, but it turned out I would never live in that house again. I drove the few miles to the trailhead that would take me into the Rattlesnake Wilderness, and started walking north. My plan was to hike into and through the Rattlesnake, cross the Jocko River, and continue north into the Mission Mountains.

I'd tried stuff like this before, but on a much smaller scale. In college one year, over spring break, I decided to take off alone and hitchhike west. I'm not sure exactly why. I suppose it was because my girlfriend and I were in the slow, uncertain midst of falling out of love. I was twenty years old and didn't know what I wanted to do with my life, and I'd been reading contemporary novels about dreamy, alienated Americans. After a day of thumbing rides, I reached the Blue Ridge Mountains where I left the highway for the woods to find a place to pitch my tent. I ate cold sandwiches. The sun went down and a rain started up. I huddled in my little tent, feeling awfully alone and miserable. It's possible that I cried. I'm sure I asked myself what the hell I was doing there. And I know I read a book by flashlight late into the night to distract myself from having to find some answer to that question. The next day I thumbed my way back home.

A lot had happened since then. I'd finished college, gone to graduate school, taken a job, quit that job, and taken another. I'd gotten married, conceived a son, and grieved my son when he died at birth. I'd experienced the satisfaction of having a community of friends emerge around me, and then experienced pained confusion as the community splintered into smaller factions. My marriage had unravelled. Two months before, my wife and I had separated. I didn't know whether we'd get back together or not. I didn't know whether I wanted to get back together or not.

The effect that all this had on me was something like a chronic version of the fleeting experiences I've had while travelling and waking up in an unfamiliar room: The furniture is strange and the daylight enters the room at an unexpected angle, and for a moment I have the panicky feeling of having no idea where I am or how I got there, of being unable to rely on my familiar instincts, of doubting my usually confident perceptions of the world around me. I felt dislocated, as though I occupied a slightly different universe from everyone else.

I found myself just filling time, distracting myself with the familiar, engaging artifacts of my everyday life. I kicked around in my office, doodling on paper and coming up with ideas. I walked around town, buying used books and CDs and bagels and bread. I sat in my basement for hours playing pinball on the computer. Some evenings I'd go for bike rides with a friend, panting hard as we climbed the hills, and drafting on each others wheels as we whizzed back down. Some evenings I'd stay at home and turn the stereo up very loud and listen to sound bouncing around in my big empty house. I'd hug my arms to my chest and squeeze my eyes shut. Eventually it got dark, and I'd go bed and sleep. It was getting me through, but it wasn't getting me anywhere.

And so I decided that I needed to really dislocate myself, to explore the feeling of being alone. I decided to disappear for a while—to head for the Mission Mountains. I packed my camping stuff and my clothes and lots of food. I took a notebook and a pencil. I took no books. I laced up my boots, and left.

The last person I saw before I embarked on my hike was a long-haired, stringy guy in 1970s-style jeans who showed up at the trailhead when I did. He ambled along in front of me. After a quarter-mile he paused and I passed him.

"Going up?" he said.

"Yeah," I said, "For a while."

The Rattlesnake Wilderness

By late afternoon, I had set up camp at the edge of Upper Twin Lake, with Stuart Peak rising above me and the late afternoon clouds looking like rain. My legs were sore, but I wanted to look around. I bushwhacked my way down to Lower Twin Lake. It was a stark, brooding place—dead trees on an island, a bare peninsula. Then the rain came down with midsummer hail, and I hunched under a tree for a while and finally beat it back to camp.

> *lay in my tent with the rain beating down and feeling very sad—missing V in a way i don't in missoula. thought of being with her in the rain in the tent up at cedar lake in the missions last summer, cooking omelettes. that was nice and sweet, looking back.*

The first morning in the mountains I woke to the sounds of birds and water. I ate breakfast on a rock with streaks of morning sun slanting through the trees and a clear sky above me. It was breezy and cold. The air was alive with gnats and mosquitoes backlit by the sun, dancing around like sparks from a fire. Dewy spider threads glistened in the branches like shining wires. I cooked up a meal of instant coffee and oatmeal.

On my second day I hiked to Sanders Lake—where I felt a familiar, powerful emotion. Only once before had I visited Sanders Lake alone. It was a day trip. I'd biked twenty miles and then hiked another five to the top of a ridge. The wind was blowing and the sun was shining, and the blue glint of Sanders Lake brought tears to my eyes. I believe I was thinking of my dead son Benjamin then.

It is easy to imagine the sense of pride that early explorers felt when they arrived at some place that appeared on none of their maps. The odd sense of possession, the sense that "this is my place." I feel that here at Sanders Lake. Not ownership, I don't mean that. Rather, it's a sense of identification, a sense of place. I feel that sense strongly.

at dinner i felt a tinge of aloneness. i do like to share this sort of thing with a woman i'm in love with. the island, the cliff, the deep valley, the lean water, the mountain goats. that's what i crave. and maybe someday i will share this experience with someone. today, tonight, i have it all to myself and there's a lot of wonderful in that too.

I walk to the northeast end of the lake, where it spills way down to Wrangle Creek below. There's a drama and an intimacy here. I sit on the rocks and scan the rocky cliff-face to the right, and suddenly: a mountain goat. Watching the goat through my binoculars I feel that sweet, clenching surge of passion. I love this place! I love the intimacy of no one here but me and the goats. I could watch mountain goats all day long: prancing up rocks, nibbling at greens, batting flies off their ears, digging in the dirt, and settling in to look out, like me, across the wide valley filling with shadow.

a certain sense of fear when i think about leaving here tomorrow and heading north. it gets harder. less certain terrain, less certain campsites. i'm not even sure where I'll spend tomorrow night. i could spend two weeks here at Sanders, but I'd feel cowardly—like i let myself, and others, down.

I dawdled around the lake in the morning before packing up. After pumping water into my bottles, I walked down the cliff-edge of the lake again and scanned the rock face. No mountain goats this morning. I scrambled up the rocks to where that one was scraping a place to lie down last night. There are tufts of mountain goat wool snagged on the branches of twisted little trees. I stuck some in my pocket. I found the scrape and felt weird about being there—like I was trespassing, like I shouldn't be here. I felt like I did one time years ago when I climbed a cliff and dropped into a kiva in an abandoned cliff dwelling in a canyon on the Navajo reservation in Arizona. It felt thrilling and intimate, but also mysteriously wrong. Some places are not for me to trample on.

> *i miss something i'm trying to figure out: not V, necessarily, but the way we were together. i miss the happy comfort of our being together. it's not that she's not here, but that that time is in the past. i'm mourning, i guess. i'm mourning the way we were with don and jennifer at little joe lake, don and i skipping stones and the smell of smoke in the air. i mourn the way we were with jack and mary, lying on the ground by stanley hot springs, telling tales and laughing. it felt so tight. now: it's gone and i mourn it.*

I began to take more notice of the sounds of evening and morning. There's a point in the evening when the sun dips below the mountains and fills the valley with shadow, and the birds come alive with sound. In the mornings I'd often wake to the raspy, thumping sounds of deer catching my scent. One morning a deer came very close, looking at the tent a while, ears twitching. Then it rasped again and bounded off.

strange how the mind works . . . this morning finally remembered the last line of that cowboy junkies song stanza: "your mind will change and your heart will lose its pain."

32 On the ridge up above Boulder Lake I look north to the sharp peaks of the Mission Mountains, and northeast to the blue pyramids of the Swan Range. But my eyes keep returning northward to the Missions.

i feel stuck—i miss the camping, the cooking, the couchtime with V. but i feel so caged, so vulnerable, so unable to be free to be happy. i don't want to lose V, but i'm afraid i will, and if i act out of that fear—like i have been—i lose myself.

I encountered a lone dayhiker at Boulder lake. He's cooking strips of salmon and heating up a blackened pot of coffee. I like the simplicity of his approach: cutoff pants, cheap shoes, an old Gatorade bottle for water, a canvas sack of some sort as a pack. He says he was supposed to meet someone here, but they didn't show. He tells me that he and a friend did a four-night trip in the Bitterroots once. They hardly saw each other, and camped together only one night. What a concept: Hike at your own pace and if you meet up, fine; if not, that's okay too. I told him I was exploring aloneness. I said, "My wife and I separated recently." He said something about this being healing.

My fifth day was a long one. Took a rest by a little creek with a view of McLeod Peak in the distance. Thought about camping there, but the sun was still high so figured I'd just plod on. My feet and legs were tired. The achilles tendons felt stretched tight and yelped with every step as I left the Rattlesnake Wilderness and trudged northeast along a forest service road that cut through the timbered slopes. I imagined myself as one of those guys who does some sort of "Walk Across America" to raise money for muscular dystrophy or something. Trudging past prairie cornfields with a flag on his pack and a practiced quote ready for the local news anchor at the next town—waiting with microphone and a corny lead-in. I walked on and on. Finally, toward evening, I camped just off the dirt road by a little creek. A breeze kicked up and fluffy seed-pods filled the sky like a fuzzy snowstorm.

The Jocko Crossing

On my sixth day, I was ready to cross the Jocko Valley and head north into the Missions. But first, I dropped out of the mountains and hitch-hiked into the little town of Seeley Lake to restock on food. The dusty frustration of attempting to thumb a ride on seldom-travelled roads reminded me again just how unromantic hitchhiking really is. But, by early afternoon I was sitting near a grocery store with my boots off under the shade of a tree, munching on a cucumber, and swigging a bottle of juice. A checker from the store came out on her lunch break and joined me, and I realized that I was starved for conversation and human contact. I found myself being unusually gregarious and interested in her stories about Yellowstone and the Old Faithful visitor center. It struck me that she probably had a son around my age. I was a conversation piece myself, of course: Where was I from? Where was I going next? I informed her I had hiked through the Rattlesnake and was about to head up into the Missions. I told her I intended to spend a couple of weeks with nobody but myself. "You better really like yourself," she said, and laughed.

Later that day I soaked my tired feet in the chilly, snow-fed waters of Jocko Creek. I lathered my sweaty body with peppermint soap and rinsed with handfuls of water. Nothing, I thought to myself, has ever felt better than this. I feel giddy from the pure physical experience of my body, of the now-ness of the cold moving river water across my calves.

But I feel too the sadness of being happy alone. No one to share it with. No one to hug or hold or high-five or to just smile at and say, "Yes, that felt great." Being happy alone makes aloneness salient.

> *felt a twinge of missing V, ignored it for a while and then found it. the sense of loss of what we had (or i thought we had). the sweetness, the joy, the easy affection and delight. i dunno if i can retrieve that, or whether the hurt runs too deep. i wonder: am i mourning the change in our relationship, or the change in me—the change from willful blindness to seeing things as they are? am i mourning who i was and how that seemed to work okay?*

The Mission Mountains

So, on the seventh day I made my way into the Mission Mountain wilderness, hiking the steep trail that would take me to Grey Wolf Lake. A couple of miles into the hike I spied a single silvery horseshoe on the trail. A couple of miles later, I came across two women on horseback.

"Are you going to Grey Wolf?" they ask.

Yes, I reply. They were planning on going there too, they tell me, to meet a couple of friends who were camping there. But it seems one of their horses had thrown a shoe. Yes, I say, I saw the shoe. So they're turning back and won't meet their friends after all.

"Would you do us a favor?" they ask, "Would you take something to our friends?"

Sure, I say. And so one of them reaches into her saddlebags and pulls out two cans of Coors from a cooler. I'm briefly amazed. I mean, here I am carrying a pack loaded down with two weeks worth of food, and they're asking me to add on twenty-four ounces of bad beer just because their horse couldn't make it to the lake! Oh well, what the hell: I said I'd do it, finding a way to fit the beer in my pack. Their friends are named Katie and Nancy. I hike on toward the lake. Of course, my heavy pack feels no heavier than before.

The approach to Grey Wolf Lake is spectacular, with long views of rocky ridges and peaks, and a steep valley with a cascading creek carving through it. At the lake I see a woman by the shoreline who waves me over and asks me if I saw two women on horseback. You must be Katie or Nancy, I say.

"I'm Nancy," she replies.

I've got something for you, I tell her, suddenly savouring the joy of being a total stranger bearing unexpected pleasures. I hand over the two cold cans of beer. Nancy, of course, is delighted. We talk for a moment.

"Would you like to have dinner with us tonight?" she asks. Yes, it turns out I would.

Dinner. The wonderful sweet-hot snap of a radish and the crunch of snow peas. The simple joy of conversation with a couple of new acquaintances on the rocky shore of a wilderness lake. We talked about the feeling of being in these mountains.

"After my divorce," Katie said, "I spent the whole summer in the Missions alone."

They had both spent decades hiking here, on trail and off. They told me of routes that once were marked on maps but no longer are, and of routes that never were marked at all. They spoke of how they like it that way.

"We kicked down cairns our whole hike up here," said Nancy.

Before darkness fell, I walked back along the lakeshore to my own tent. The delicious dessert of brushing my teeth.

I sat up late, watching the stars come out. I focused on a silent satellite crawling across the sky when suddenly—catching the light of the long-gone sun—it glowed brightly for a second, like a burning ember.

In the morning it rained, so I holed up in my tent. I did a little mending of pants and jacket. Mosquitoes swarmed against the screen.

Time passed at a rate I couldn't figure out at all. I stared at my map, lingering on mountains and lakes to come, tracing possible bushwhacking routes off-trail, wondering just where I might go when I leave Grey Wolf Lake. I felt a passion, an excitement, to move through valleys and across passes, to find my way via unmarked routes, to explore the unknown.

> *i learned something yesterday: i need to ask for what i want. to trust the assumption that others know their boundaries enough to say no if want to say no, to be willing to hear 'no,' and so to ask straightaway. i gotta know my boundaries better, and to trust others to know theirs. i gotta ask for what i want.*

I lay in my tent, considering my next move. It's possible, I was told, to bushwhack one's way around the north side of Grey Wolf Lake, climb up to the Pass of the Winds, and drop down to High Park Lake. There's supposed to be a small open spot to pitch a tent at the site. And from there it's possible to scramble up over Goat Pass to Lost Lake. Sounds exciting—all off-trail and so remote and romantic. It also feels scary for some reason. It feels like a test—like some test of my strength to go it alone, to face up to my fears of finding a way up and down that steep rocky unknown. I decide I'll do a dayhike today to check out the route—to hike the uncertain terrain packless to see whether I want to risk turning an ankle with a full load on my back.

I remembered a dream I'd had a few times over the past month or two. A dream in which I'm standing at the top of a rocky cliff and I have to somehow find my way down. I feel terrified and a little stupid. As I sit in my tent, the dream seems very real and prescient, loaded with murky self-symbolism. It was time to strap on my boots.

By midday I've crested the Pass of the Winds. I stand on hardened cornices of snow, looking southeast across Grey Wolf Lake and northeast across High Park Lake. To the north is Goat Peak and, hidden behind the ridge, Lost Lake. I have already decided: I won't go there. The climb just to get here was scrambly, the footing uncertain. Maybe I'll do that another time with a lighter pack. But not tomorrow; tomorrow I'll strike out on a different route. It's an emotional decision: Am I giving in? Am I failing my symbolic test? Am I backing down out of fear? No, I feel okay about it. I'm playing it smart. I'm making sure I don't get carried away by the idealized romance of who I am and what I need to do. I'm backing down from the challenge physically, but I feel successful mentally. I shrewdly looked it over, I thought it through, and I made an intelligent choice. I choose to remain safe and smart. I have my limits.

> *thinking about benjamin as i hiked back down from the pass. i mourn but i'm not sure just what i mourn. it's confusing. not sure what thoughts, wishes, losses, whatever to attach to the feeling of sadness and pain that grips me when i feel his death.*

The sun dips over the ridge between Grey Wolf Peak and Three

Summit Peak. It's very still. No breeze at all, and I get the eerie sense of a weather change about to occur. Low clouds roll in like a fog from the southwest, obscuring the peaks around the lake. Intensely lovely with the low sun glinting against the clouds from below.

Grey Wolf Lake feels like a home of sorts—a resting place in the middle of a restless time. A place to feel part of. I've spent three days at Grey Wolf Lake and it scares me a little to think of packing up and moving on tomorrow.

i still have moments of wanting to go back immediately to missoula, but i've passed the real trouble now. i know and feel the rhythm. in a sense, it really does not feel like 9 days. i mean, there has been no plot, no clear action to make it seem like time passing. all i've done is hike, camp, think, feel, read a bit, talk a bit, write a lot, and sleep at night.

I sit on a rock in the still air, by the calm water of Crystal Lake, watching the descending sun play flickery tricks against the sky. Behind me, to the east, the sky is a light evening blue. Westward, the sky is grey roiling clouds and behind them it is bright white. I watch the cycle of the clouds as they move eastward: forming, growing, and then disappearing again. Two loons dive and reappear thirty meters away. A family of ducks paddle in a line—the ducklings straggling, then fluttering to catch up.

Another day, another hike northward. Bushwhacked my way over a ridge and down a thick slope to Glacier Creek. Scratches on my legs, twigs in my socks, and pine needles in my shorts. My body feels itchy and dirty and good. I immerse my whole body in the shallow creek, gasping hard as I thrust my head under the cold rushing water.

i think of her flaws, her weaknesses that make it impossible for me now to . . . i dunno, i just feel the confusion of sadness and pain and love and longing and loss. i'm glad the river is roaring around me, and secretly hoping some unsuspecting stranger will wander down this little path to find me doubled up, holding my sides, my cheeks soaked, my nose running, and do something or say something that will be like magic and my heart will lose it's pain. ("come here," she said, "there's plenty of room in my iron bed . . .")

It seems to take mere moments to hike to Heart Lake, and I set up camp there with the sun still in the morning sky. In the afternoon I scrambled up past Island Lake to the ridgetop and looked over the other side to Cliff Lake and MacDonald Peak rising snowy and dramatic above it. To the north I see the craggy peak of Calowahcan in the far distance. My map tells me that Summit Lake is there, and that's my destination for tomorrow. Most of it, I know, will be a true bushwhack off-trail. It's a bit scary. I think I could just hike back down and out instead. But I won't. Tomorrow will be hard, this I know.

The brutal joy of hiking off-trail. Bushwhacking strong and fast past Cheff Lake, past Loco Lake. The mosquitos are thick. Sometimes I follow a creek, sometimes I just point northward and crash through thickets of brush and scramble across slopes of beargrass. Sometimes I find a game-trail and follow it until it splinters and disappears. Sometimes I think I find a dusty piece of trail only to discover that it's just the decayed remains of a long-dead toppled tree, returning to the earth. Above Spider Lake I find a thin remnant of a trail among the glacier lilies, and I follow it down to a string of snowy pools where I lose it again. I power straight up a talus slide to the top of the ridge. I feel as strong as a goat. Eventually I pick up a path and lose it, and thrash my way down to Frog Lakes, where I find a marked trail and follow it to Summit Lake. Then I strip and swim out away from the mosquitos, with the snowy crags of Calowahcan rising above me.

I sit in the late afternoon sun, my feet in the water, washing my shorts. There is a thudding sound behind me. I turn and catch a flash of white twenty feet away. A mountain goat, all woolly and curious. Beside her, a kid, like a lamb, cute and snubnosed and as white—of course—as snow. I shift. They stop and look at me. Suddenly the kid bleats and runs off down the shoreline. The mom bleats too, lingers a moment, and then runs off.

I take inventory of my food. Enough for two dinners, two breakfasts. I could descend into the valley and hitchhike to a store and buy more provisions. It's tempting. But no, I decide I'll eat what I've got and then head back to Missoula, to return to the life of people. I'm excited as I think about it. Yet, I realize that I don't want this trip to end. It's easy up here. It's scary to go back.

I miss the trail up Elk Pass, so I bushwhack straight up the slope.

Pushing quickly, pantingly, flailing my arms at the mosquitoes that haze around me. Batting at my head, my shoulders. At the top of the pass I find the trail. A wind blows the mosquitoes off and I catch my breath and clean their black sodden bodies from my arms and from where they mix with sweat behind my ears.

I make my way toward Mollman Lakes. I'd been there once before, just one summer ago with V. We'd camped at Upper Mollman Lake in the warm August sun. It occurs to me that that was the last time she and I backpacked together. I wonder whether it seems too planful, too symbolic of something (I don't know what) for me to spend the last two nights of this journey at the very same lake. But no, I decide, it's simpler than that. I'm going to Mollman Lakes because, well, because they're right here and so am I.

As I crest the notch at Mollman Lakes I smell woodsmoke faintly. Is it real? Is there a campsite somewhere that I don't see? Or do I merely smell my own jacket? Or is it an illusion, a smell in my brain that yearns for those things that the smell of woodsmoke suggests: warmth and coziness, easy laughter and quiet musings, uncomplicated companionship.

i came here to cry but i'm not crying. i cried as i hiked up the notch to the lakes from the basin below, with the wind whipping cold against me, and me feeling not strong like a goat today, but kinda weak—cold and tired and more than a little human as i made my way to this spot as i knew i would. but i'm not crying now.

Sitting on a rock in the sun by Upper Mollman Lake. The mass of grey clouds blows past and the sun comes out and there's the familiar white, puffy clouds fleeting overhead against the blue. It's chilly. I rinse my sweaty, dirty clothes in the lake. Socks, windpants, T-shirt, bandanna. I slop water on my chest and under my arms and kneel forward into the cold lake to wash my hair. The mosquitos are laying low in the breeze and not bothersome at all. I've done a few idle errands—a bit of sewing, some gathering of firewood—but I'm not straying far from this rock by the lake. I could hike out today, but I won't. I have food for one more day. This is a day of rest. Tomorrow I will descend happily into the life of people. Today I will spend happily in the mountains.

On my last night in the Mission Mountains I had a dream. I was returning home from this trip and encountered my father. He told me how, during my time away, the grasses and plants became dry and brittle, and he thought they were dead until it rained all day and they grew green again. In my dream I felt at first a twinge of complicated guilt, as though it were my fault. But then my feeling of guilt went away. I had the sense that, hey, I did my best; and besides, everything turned out okay after all. When I awoke, I thought about that part of me that I tend to idealize, that part that wants to be above reproach, to be perfect and good and honest and giving and all things to all people. I shook my head at it all. Gotta chip away at those ideals a bit, I thought to myself.

I also found myself thinking about olive bread. I think I dreamed of olive bread again last night.

Returning

I hiked out of the Missions and began to walk west on Mollman Trail road, past the first litterings of houses with their cheap roofs, barking dogs, hulks of cars and trucks abandoned in the weeds. The gravel crunched under my boots and stretched out before me for three miles to the highway, hot and bright and dusty and straight as a map edge. The side of the road was lined with the dusty green and flashing purple of flowering knapweed, and fluttering all around me were hundreds of butterflies. I stopped briefly and chatted over the fence with a rancher.

"Been up in the mountains?" he asked. I told him where I'd been.

"Sounds like a good hike," he said.

Fragments of Potential

Cheryl Lousley

Prologue

THE DEW SOAKS THROUGH MY RUNNING SHOES AS I RACE WITH the dog across the back field to our spot overlooking the creek. Early morning is the best time to catch sight of the beaver swimming above the dam and I slow as we reach the fence, stilling my heavy breaths, approaching quietly, reverently. A morning mist hovers over the water and I do not see the v-shaped wake of the swimming beaver. The water is still. Silent. This perch is like a window into another world, and I hesitate before pushing on. Hesitant, perhaps, to trespass into the home of the forest creatures. In summer the water is shallow enough that I wade through the swirls of minnows, crunching over shells, slipping often on the slimy seaweed. Accompanied by a book, my journal, and a pen, I pass a lazy Sunday afternoon on the rocky "beach," only exposed in late

July and August, watching the cedar waxwings flit back and forth from tree to tree overhead. The bright colours of the meadow wildflowers—yellows, purples, blues, whites—dull in autumn. I collect milkweed and grapevine, twisting it into wreaths and leaving them hanging to dry in the trees—benevolent signs of human presence to others passing through. The creek turns into a skating rink come January and then becomes so covered in snow I must snowshoe. Only then can I fully explore all the twists and turns and inlets of the creek, following deer tracks into a cedar grove or finding rabbit tracks gathered around a water hole. For years I have followed the passing of seasons at the creek, though it has not been my physical home since I was a young child.

Introduction

Some days I feel overwhelmed by powerlessness, by fear of the difficulties ahead, by changes I cannot stop; I feel angry at the injustices dismissed under the rhetoric of globalization; I feel sad and discouraged when I see a world of emptiness, pollution, and violence surrounding me. Some days I just want to go home, walk down to the creek and listen to the leaves falling on the ground. I want to pick the last few wildflowers in the field and celebrate autumn. I have the privilege to be pursuing graduate studies, but I wonder what good will another lecture, another discussion, another rally do? And so I write. I write in anger and desperation, I write with joy, with nostalgia. I write without purpose and to an audience of no one. These are my journals, fragments from my early twenties. Journals, the place where I house my dreams, desires, and visions of somehow claiming—learning—coming—home again one day. Knowing I cannot.

All I ask of the reader is a response. Some response. Any response. I just can't bear indifference right now.

I: Spring

This is the first time I have been home since the ice-storm devastated eastern Ontario, leaving my folks and neighbours without water, heat, or electricity for more than two weeks. The over-the-phone descriptions of the damage could not prepare me for the sadness I felt when I saw the trees, beheaded, bent over to the ground, split open with gaping wounds. We could see through the woods to houses, roads, creeks never visible before.

I left springtime in Toronto—strangely come in February, where students roller-blade through the university campus, where Queen Street West is flooded with strolling shoppers, where an early morning walk brings a chorus of singing birds, rushing cars, and crisp air—to tour stretches of snowy fields littered with branches. Another world. The extended community from all the farms and roads around the village gathered in the church hall on Saturday for the Ham Supper. I chatted with neighbours I had not seen for months, sometimes years, or newcomers I had not met before. Washing up the dishes afterwards, I answered questions about what I was currently doing, where I was living. Practical questions. I tried to explain what sort of job I could get after completing my master's degree in education. So much I cannot explain in this setting.

It's like last spring when the piano tuner came by. I was studying, working on some papers, and had slipped home for some quiet space to write. As he worked, he liked to chat, and so I heard all about his sons, what each was doing now and the practical choices involved, about where they must go to find work, the uncertainties. I am so awkward at such moments. It's a language I never learned and I feel my inadequacy (probably interpreted as snobbery) with every social interaction out here. Out there. Six years (and counting) of university study have only widened that gap.

How do I say that I am in school because I love to study, not to pursue a prudent career path? How do I say that I study environmental education in full knowledge of its bleak employment prospects? How do I say I was never looking for that kind of job anyway? How do I say that I place idealism, politics, personal interest first? How do I explain to my rural community what I mean by an academic community? How do I say I never plan to marry or to raise children? How do I say that I am vegetarian? How do I deal with my privilege to have travelled, to have studied, to feel secure enough to not yet worry about employment?

How could I live here again?

In the city, people ask me how I came to be so concerned about environmental issues, why am I so motivated—angry—committed—passionate? And I answer that it comes from here, my rural origins, from years of watching the stars of the night sky during the walk back to the house after evening chores; from a childhood of running my fingers through the grain-like grasses along the roadside and sucking the sweetness from the pink clover in the field; from crouching under a heat lamp, bottle-feeding a new-born lamb, the musky smell of sheep filling the barn. From blissful, giddy days running in the fields, collecting buckets of minnows from the creek, doing barn chores, rolling the hay off the wagon before I was big enough to lift a bale on my own.

But we are not really rural people. My parents bought our farm when they married and pursued farming part-time, as a complement to their professional jobs. And though I was born here, I have already spent more of my life away than living here. From an early age, I was more interested in burying my head in books than my fingers in the soil. It often seems that my environmentalism is an attempt to recover what I have lost in that process—loss of home, place, community, language, childhood, innocence.

This is not something I can explain out here because the land, the community, it's all still here. The loss is in me. I have romanticized my own background.

I drop the token in, smile good morning to the attendant at the window. Waiting for the subway train to arrive, I try to read, standing against the wall. Some days I just watch people, or sit idle. Thinking, or not thinking. But then I feel guilty—I should be using this valuable time to read—and I dutifully bring along a book for the hour-long TTC trek out to York University from downtown Toronto. Even after a term of such weekly trips, I still feel queasy, stomach unsettled, on arrival.

Suburbia.

Today I make the trip to help with an environmental education conference for teachers and students from local high schools. The day passes by in fragments of conversations, listening, writing, speaking. I hear myself talking about environmental justice, about the need to engage topics such as accessible and sustainable transportation options in city planning, or the class, race, and gender dimensions of exposure to pollution, toxins, and hazardous waste in the workplace, home, and community. But they want to hear about planting trees and gardens, about animals and plants and wild spaces, about sunshine and water and fishing and hiking. And I wonder: am I deadening nature for them? Am I turning their sense of wonder, inspiration, excitement into just another issue, another subject? Is the politicization empowering or depressing? Do I not think back to my creek whenever I need inspiration? Is that a privilege I am denying them?

I rethink all my priorities, layering critique upon critique, hoping one day to reconcile them. Or, perhaps just accept the contradictions, not pushing too hard to understand.

Sunshine. I tramp out in the muddy, wet remains of the winter snow to snip some pussy willows. I follow the path of high ground shaped a century ago as a dam for the mill pond. Mill Pond Farm. My father bought each of us a tacky blue-and-white baseball cap with "Mill Pond Farm" inscribed on the front. I shoved mine somewhere far to the back of the closet in my bedroom, as appreciative of it as I am of early Saturday morning wake-ups calls to help a neighbour with the haying, or shovelling out a chicken coop.

The birds are singing and the warmth of the sun is bringing the frozen landscape back to life. The dog runs up with her stick and I give in to her play, laughing as we make our way to the creek's edge, water oozing into the toes of my boots. The creek's running fast and high and we watch the debris of winter sweep by, shivering with the still-cool breeze coming off the water.

On the way back, I find the pussy willow tree I seek out each spring, now indistinctive among the leafless brush. The pussy willows are just beginning to peek out of their covers, perfect for opening in the warmth of the house. I step into the large puddle that surrounds the tree and trim a few branches for my mother to place on the table. Our land is mostly wetland and is becoming more and more so with the beavers, so it's not uncommon for the dog and me to both reappear at the house with muddy, dripping feet after one of our jaunts in the back.

I bike out to High Park to find out about its naturalization program. I have been a city cyclist for three years now, first in Hamilton, now in Toronto. The speed, the danger, the intense alertness city cycling demands always gives me an adrenaline boost. Discovering this thrill has been instrumental in helping me learn these cities, their geography, their neighbourhoods, their local cultures, their wild spaces. Toronto. Before it was all just cityness—a general category—fast-moving cars and fast-moving people, dust, grey, steel, glass, cement. Cityness. Now I'm beginning to see neighbourhoods and character and even nature within the city, learning the boundaries aren't so rigid after all.

I pass shops and restaurants—parks and bridges—cars lining the street—pulling in and out—doors opening—taxis cutting ahead—crosswalks—women with grocery bags—streetcar tracks—apartment buildings—banks—graffiti—seagulls—subway stops—theatres—a drunk lurching across the street; I watch, helpless, scared. Children behind fences, trapped on tarmac. They gather in clusters to talk and eat lunch, some kick a ball around, but I see them clutching at the fence, staring out at me, sad, longing.

I break from the chaos of Bloor Street West and enter the groomed avenues of High Park, finding my contact at the greenhouses. He gives me a tour and then invites me to join the volunteer stewardship group. More importantly, I am welcome to bring along the high school students I am working with. The dirt is piled high on the tables and its dusty smell fills the air. I feel that urge to dig my hands in deep, to get the soil good and moist and knead the earth through my fingers. I first rediscovered this pleasure when I volunteered with a Butterfly Garden as part of a university course. It was like therapy: one afternoon a week on my knees in the warm sun planting Buddleia, asters, Coreopsis, and St. Johnswort eased all my stress. Milkweed, wild bergamot, Queen Anne's Lace, and Black-eyed Susans lined the shoreline of the marsh, and I often went just to sit, to read. I also took an ecology course that term and the Saturday I spent in hipwaders taking water samples in the marsh breathed a happiness into me that lasted for weeks.

And so again I seek out this manual work to complement my otherwise very disconnected, urban studies. I commit to coming out to the next volunteer meeting.

The landscape from the train window is familiar, though I've never travelled this route before. The long, straight fields, the low mountains; it is the silos which seem most natural: strong and solemn against the purplish sky. The fields pass by pass by pass by. It's still so brown this spring—the trees stand barren, the cattails gone to seed and stagnant on their stalks, the ground waiting to be turned over, the mountains grey. The train goes on—past parking-lot-ringed industrial fortresses, past rows of houses, some so close I can see the flickering blue of their TV sets. We go on—past canteens sporting shoddy neon signs, past small town steeples, past stretches of dull meadows and flashing railway crossings. A red Massey Ferguson bailer in front of a decaying barn.

Lying on the grass, enjoying the sunshine, what special moments spring brings—like the pulsing ribbons of snow geese that flew overhead this afternoon. I've never seen anything like it in my life: long, staggering lines of geese stretching on and on into the distance only to be followed by another such pattern and another. Constantly in motion, changing places, moving ever forward, like a ribbon slowly twisting over in the hands of the gods.

II: Summer

I have been troubled this week by the insecurity and challenges of the future—whether it be what to do this summer or what to do after I finish my undergraduate degree or what this female soul desires for her Life (but isn't that Romantic project passé?). I feel a little lost, bewildered: a domesticated animal about to be set free. Yet another cliché.
I want at least some vague sense of direction. (Direction for the sake of direction?)

I feel so young at times. And then also like I am old enough that I should be DOING, LIVING, not just thinking, proposing, postponing. I feel I must rush before there is nothing left. And what is there now? Here I am, disillusioned and disappointed with academia, yet still yearning for that world of ideas, still dreading the monotony of regular work. Escaping responsibility?

I feel so inexperienced, blundering along, not even knowing where to go to gain more knowledge and skills. Not even sure that's what I'm lacking. The future bears down on me oppressively and I am frightened, intimidated. Homesick.

There is this burden of empty space ahead of me—a life to fill, to plan, to do.

The wind whips the door from my hand as I leave the house and slams it shut, the window left vibrating from the impact. In a burst of thunder, the sky, the house, and ground shake together beneath me, around me. I stand alone in the darkness, my feet buried in a warm carpet of grass. Another time I would have been chilled by the cool summer temperature. Now I am calm and still. Expectant.

The wind dances around me, blowing my hair back from my face and my night-shirt against my body. I close my eyes, yielding to the coming storm. Leaves shower off the cherry tree in a steady stream and I fly with them in the wind. The sunflower stalks sway, rustling beside me. The house creaks and shifts and the night is alive with noises and movements. Pitch black, the pasture has become the unknown, cloaking wandering animals and spirits that now seem so close, so present. A coyote howl? Or my imagination?

I open my eyes as the darkness is broken by a wild flash of lightning. The dark storm clouds tower over me and I feel humbled. Insignificant. The darkness returns and I watch and wait, excited by the flowing energy. More flashes of lightning follow the first until the wind suddenly dies down and the night becomes still.

I hurry over to let the dog out of her pen, now feeling the cold all through my body. We rush inside and as I crawl into bed, the sky crashes once more and the rain begins to fall.

The first day of summer and a hot and heavy one at that. I just couldn't sit in the office—the sunshine and my graduate-school application weighed on my mind. So I got the application in and now I'm lounging on a grassy slope in the park in the coolness of the close of the day. The clink of a baseball bat echoes among the chorus of crickets and birds, a steady vehicle rumble always the backdrop.

I can't read the newspaper some days. The violence becomes just too much. Too much. Page after page—it just can't be absorbed, comprehended—how can I respond? We have not been taught how to respond; we just adapt somehow to this environment of information overload, of violence, of cruelty, of speed, of superficial omnipresence, now called globalization.

How can I respond to such a world? personally? academically? politically? I ask this question because I need to respond. I'd rather not know than give up responding. I stubbornly refuse to admit powerlessness. Yet it takes its toll on my spirit, I know it does. Fellow students ask why I have to make everything so political. Why talking to me has to make them sad, or depressed, or angry. I'm always aiming for the latter, hoping anger will push them to act, to scream, to protest. But I respond more with depression, with hopelessness, than with anger. I yearn to slip away to my creek.

And sometimes I do just that. Mostly, I turn to organizing—joining groups, supporting causes, seeking out information from the alternative press—hoping the community of activists will keep my spirits up, keep me going. But the series of meetings, discussions, letters, begins to blur and seems like frantic activity rather than action. Do we keep moving to disguise our lack of influence and effect? Or are my expectations just too high and my commitment too weak?

I met a man in the photocopy shop yesterday who appeared like a messenger, just as I was slowing down, losing momentum. Noticing "environment" at the top of an article I was having copied for one of my classes, he addressed me quietly: "You know the problem isn't about trees."

"I know," I answered. And we went on to talk about environmental ethics, global inequalities, resource privatization, and the IMF.

As I paid for my copies and turned to leave, he looked me straight in the eye and said, "We're talking about struggle." "Struggle," he repeated. "You can get married, have kids and a nice middle class life if you want." I nod, knowing what he will say next. "But what we need is individuals who will continue to struggle for change." Again I nod. "You are still so young. Ten years of dedicated activism and you will still have your life ahead of you."

Ten years!?

I try another sort of initiative: a positive, exciting, even fun kind of project which we call "ecomusee." For a year and a half we meet—a group of academics, teachers, amateur historians, naturalists, students—and plan community walks around Hamilton in an effort to rekindle some sort of sense of place and local knowledge in the city. In some ways, the initiative was a great success. One warm August evening seventy people gathered in West Hamilton's Victoria Park, former site of the 1860s Crystal Palace fairgrounds, for a walk through the Strathcona and Hess Village neighbourhoods. A geography student and an amateur historian guided the group past Ontario cottages, old factory sites, and red-brick row houses, up to the large, detached residences (some still with carriage houses) originally lived in by the factory owners atop Burlington Heights. Of course, many others on the walk also had stories to tell: a local resident mentioned that a church we were passing housed a stained-glass window by Group of Seven artist Frank Carmichael. While caught by surprise, the minister of the Korean congregation that now worships in the church was delighted in having the group, in tens and twelves, enter and view the window. And on we went—a jovial swarm of seventy—through the neighbourhood until the walk was brought to a close at a pub in trendy Hess Village, new friends made, old stories remembered, a neighbourhood explored. Criticism from a black-heritage activist and the de-politicization of our goals into family heritage walks dampened my enthusiasm, as did the frustration of organizing as a committee. But I remained committed until other forces dictated a move to Toronto.

(But now, years later, I hear one morning on my radio that the amateur historian has been brutally stabbed to death. He knew so many people—touched so many lives—that the report extends beyond some back-page paragraph to the Toronto news and the announcer somehow sounds confused about passing along this bit of "news" about this unknown person . . . isn't the news supposed to be about important things?)

Restless, with time to spare, I went for an exploratory bike ride through the vast grounds of the Hamilton cemetery. How beautiful! with two young girls wandering through the gravestones, exclaiming their finds; with elegant, tall, full-bodied trees and blooming tiger lilies; and, of course, with a melody of birds whose songs I have never learned. Intrigued by a downward path, arched with vines and trees, I descended to the peaceful sunken gardens, then promptly collected my bike and myself and crossed the railway tracks to climb above Highway 403, overlooking Cootes Paradise marsh. If it were not for the noise, it would have been a charming spot to watch the sun set over the water. Feeling exposed above the highway, I did not stay to write but retraced my steps—returned home—but was till not content. I play the piano for an hour. It feels good to let my fingers work the keys, smoothly, gently flying from note to note, caught up in the melody and forgetting all else.

III: Autumn

I attended a lecture on Red Hill Valley and the proposed expressway last week, wrote it up in an article for the student newspaper, but also felt the need to get out and explore the area myself. So, early this morning, before sunrise, S-- and I went for a hike along the creek.

I couldn't get over how this natural area was right in the middle of the city, literally off the busline: the cars rush by as we descend the trail. Off the busline: how strange! Perhaps it is appropriate, though, a testimony to a natural history elsewhere buried under pavement. And yet once we descended into the valley, at the base of Albion Falls, it was as intimate and private as my creek at home. The city melted away, except for a few jarring reminders scattered about in remnants of garbage and graffiti-covered vehicles.

An expressway was proposed for this site over thirty years ago and now it is about to be funded by the new provincial government. Imagine opposing a project for thirty years! Researching, lobbying, making presentations, gathering support—sustaining all that energy, continuing all those activities, not to mention all the time, money and emotional commitment involved in citizens' initiatives. For thirty years, always on the verge of losing or winning; with periods of down-time, when the project is stalled or awaiting some committee meeting, with periods of anxiety, waiting, waiting for decisions. They say that the temperature of downtown Hamilton could rise by two to three degrees if this greenery is replaced with asphalt and cars. They say the wetland at the mouth of the creek plays a crucial role in filtering out pollutants from entering Hamilton Harbour. They say the valley is home to fifteen species of fish, forty-seven species of butterflies, seventy-two species of birds of which twenty-eight breed in the valley, forty species of mammals, eleven species of amphibians. They say all this but it means little until I come here.

Red Hill Creek is the last free-flowing creek running into the Hamilton Harbour; all the others have been rerouted, buried, stopped up, directed into human-made channels. Somehow it is this last vestige of wildness that makes Red Hill worth saving, that makes its loss such a tragedy, more than just another environmental assessment, another greenspace lost to development, another highway.

They say the proposal is the result of backroom deals with real estate developers, that it is not in the public interest.

By the end of our hike, all I could feel was that the valley is a sad strip of nature crowded in by the city. My heart aches for this lonely creek that no one seems to care about—it's out of place (but of course the creek is the only thing here that is NOT out of place), neglected. In a twisted sort of way I thought maybe I could understand the argument that an expressway would improve the area.

Discouraging.

We didn't see many birds—thought we would at that time of the morning, but it was cold, September now, and perhaps I wasn't really paying attention, off in my own thoughts.

I have just come from a department reception and I'm feeling particularly pessimistic and scared and useless and lonely.

So much negative, so much complication, so many empty words.

Everything gets confused.

I wonder why I try—what I'm doing here, why I study, why I have nothing to say but spiral inward and spout empty words.

Why write? There are libraries full of books.

What can I do?

There is so much to do and it is all impossible.

Give up, get a job, buy a life (as if it was as easy as it is distasteful).

My head aches.

The wine? Or the pessimism?

I am tired. Tired at the age of twenty.

I just want to go home, walk down to the creek and listen to the leaves fall to the ground. I just want to pick the last few wildflowers in the field and celebrate autumn. I want to watch the sun rise and the sun set and the stars come out and the moon rise with no one around but the dog. And sing quietly to myself.

I sit in the stark light of a bare, sterile kitchen in this Toronto Annex house I share with three other young women. I listen to a CBC report on American government involvement in detention camps (torture, execution) in Guatemala and the subsequent cover-up (attempted—they fired and charged the man who followed his conscience and revealed the truth).

I literally shake at my fear of that overwhelming, destructive—omnipotent—power. POWER. I live from day to day by pushing out all these things I know (and have avoided knowing in more depth)—the human rights abuses; the genocides; the tortures; refugees; the poverty imposed on people worldwide through a system and policies that reward the rich, take away land, means of subsistence, family, community, human bonding; the destruction of our environment, our lifeline. It goes on and on and on and I think if we could just change, just focus our priorities on LIFE instead (but then who's we? who is creating this crisis? who is benefiting from it? who is making the decisions here? I cannot absolve myself but the thought of change seems to be such naive idealism) then all would get better but what I REALLY do is intentionally, wilfully FORGET.

I want to ask someone: how do you go on living—eating, sleeping, doing all those things that fill our daily lives—when the knowledge becomes too heavy?

I wander down to the creek with the dog. It's a cool October afternoon and we're out for a breath of air after the long Thanksgiving meal. The leaves had all blown off the trees before I got home last night, so everything looks bare, prepared for winter. We poke about our usual spots, but the wind is brisk and the day silent.

Tomorrow I catch the train back to Toronto.

IV: Winter

The snow crunches with each step. Self-absorbed, I have to stop to hear the life around me.

In the open, the whiteness gives such freedom. I want to run, laugh, jump over a log, tumble onto the snow. I want to throw myself down, roll in the snow, tossing it up and over me, burrowing in just like my dog when we go for winter walks.

Geometric figures glow yellow between the trees, fusing snow and sunlight into a frozen landscape, broken by the *rat tat tat tat* of a woodpecker and the crunching boots of a wandering girl.

I went for a long, exploratory cross-country ski in Cootes. I just set out—eager to enjoy the snow—not knowing where I was going, where I wanted to go. So I followed this trail for a while, then broke off to another, then changed direction.

Out on the ice, the wind was blowing strong, smoothing away all evidence of previous skiers until I was there alone, warm in the sunlight. I paused to catch my breath and smiled—just smiled, happy—leaning on my ski poles, looking around and around at the distant shorelines. I've never seen Cootes from the centre of the marsh before: now I feel more at home here. Before I was always at the edge, sticking to that fringe of forest and to the common trails, watching the birds out on the water, watching the canoeists, watching the biology project all from the sidelines.

I followed a skier back to the shore above Princess Point, climbed the hill, and worked my way back to school—leaving white for park for houses for streets.

It's like a blizzard outside my window—the snow swirling white, gently darkening the morning. I play one song over and over again. Not knowing why, knowing it draws me under. I like the sadness, the sinking, the confused tremor. Melancholy is addictive, a narcotic.

The trinkets on the desk pass before my wandering eyes—the clutter of day-to-day business. Meaningless, useless, but somehow necessary—as if to prove activity—worthwhile activity—is taking place here. That we're being productive.

Every goddamn second.

An afghan lies crumpled, bunched, hanging off the bed—the only true evidence of life—spontaneous life. The only object not planned, not carefully placed. The empty cocoon, softly lit by an overhanging lamp, is freshly abandoned. The cover thrown off, the pillow still expectant, primed and ready, though used. The spot lies bare but the space speaks life: emotion curled a girl under that warmth; life threw the afghan aside, limp and forgotten. Itself almost like a tender, fragile body, exhausted and sleeping.

I have moved to the window, my familiar haunt. Cuddling a cup of tea, warmed by the heat, I listen to the wind, staring out into the blackness—the sparsely lit streets, the freedom they embody, walking in the air in the wide expanse of silence, singing, humming. No. Singing and laughing and dancing.

I have a dream—of a young woman walking down her laneway, a dog at her heels, a basket on her arm. It is early summer—but dry and the fields are slightly brown, dulled in the afternoon sun. A whistling breeze brings some air across the farm and blows her white dress fluttering about her legs, tight to her body, moving through her—with her. She breathes in the wind and in the hazy glimmer the boundaries fuzz. The scene is one of orchestrated beauty—music flowing through the sky, the body, the cloth, the dirt, the fields until, without breaking the rhythm, her simple steps show it all to be but a summer afternoon.

I have a dream—of a girl picking her way along the shore of a creek.

But we've heard all this before.

The wind is dying down.

The veil of warm melancholy lifts and the room is crass, cold, empty. Wasted.

Postscript

I'm not satisfied. You sway from enthusiasm to melancholy, from joy to gloom. Hope. Despair. But there's something missing, some bigger point. I feel drained from the rush of emotion and now frustrated: we haven't arrived at anything, any place. You have questions but no answers. Fragments but no vision. I don't want to end up in Disneyland, but I wonder where you want to take the reader—I think there's more potential than just a fleeting moment.

IT'S NOT WASTED DAMMIT. I refuse to submit to this ending.

Slaughterhouse

How Vandals Destroyed My Home and What I Did About It

J. Douglas Porteous

MY VILLAGE HAS BEEN SLAUGHTERED, STEAMROLLERED, SMASHED. The centre of the earth, for me, is gone. I am profoundly place-less; I can't go home again. In its place are warehouses, yards, and wharves: an industrial park, as park-like as the surface of the moon. Economic force, not fate, destroyed this place. People with the upper hand—company directors, politicians, and bureaucrats—did it in. People concerned with profit, power, and plans, not people concerned about people. I'd like to tell you about me, about my village, about its annihilation and what this means, and what I've tried to do about it.

Where I've Been

My father was a railway plumber, my mother the village postmistress. I lived among an extended family, with a family tree rooted in the swampy landscape of Howdenshire, East Yorkshire, since the fourteenth century. We were rooted, then rooted up.

Some members of my family were ambitious. My turn came with the various post-war British Education Acts, providing free schooling even unto the PhD. My father died when I was sixteen, whereupon my mother became the proverbial poor widow. Like Jack, I had to go out and make good. A taste for learning, facilitated by British socialism, enticed me from my comfortable rural backwater, up the beanstalk, to the dizzy heights and glittering prizes of Oxford, Hull, Harvard, and MIT. Then it was Vietnam Time and, once my US student visa ran out, I was liable for the draft. I crossed the border to the sanity of Victoria, British Columbia, where I've taught in the geography department of the University of Victoria for over thirty years.

I undertook, from the late 1970s, to bring the humanities back into geography and social science, whence they had been long since banned in favour of quantification, abstruse theory, and a pragmatic turn towards supplying the needs of government and business. The humanistic approach provokes fundamental questioning. I began to pursue issues of environmental subjectivity—aesthetics, ethics, spirituality, and attachment to place. I teach a couple of off-the-wall courses (for social science): "Environmental Aesthetics" and "Landscapes of the Heart."

And it's landscapes of the heart that I want to talk of here. The chief of these is "home," at once a simple and yet an immeasurably complex concept. This isn't the "home" of real estate (a lying language) but the place(s) where one's heart is. Whether we like it or not (and often not, in our teens), home for most of us is the most meaningful place on the surface of the earth. It doesn't have to be a dwelling, it can be a place, a landscape, or all three.

I have three homes. One's a tiny wooden shack in the forest on Saturna Island, British Columbia. Here I can commune with nature: close encounters with eagles, vultures, herons, ravens, hummingbirds, and robins, deer, racoons, and otters, Douglas firs, arbutus, cedars, the great rushing riptide at Boat Pass, and that little garlic-smelling mushroom that grows on the undersides of fallen salal leaves. But I work in Victoria, so there I have an equally small apartment, but with a magnificent view of ships and blue sea, and the mauve and snowy Olympic mountains across the Juan de Fuca Strait in the good ol' USA.

The smallness of Saturna Island, with three hundred people, reconstitutes the small size of my childhood East Yorkshire village. The view across the strait, magnified fifty times, is the view from my childhood bedroom window across the richly chocolate-coloured River Ouse to the alien shores of West Yorkshire, where things are different.

Yes, I'm fixated on my third home, my ancestral village of Howdendyke, East Yorkshire, England, the British Isles, Europe, the World, the Solar System, the Galaxy, the Universe. That village, and my family's house in it, remains my still point in the turning world, my centre of the earth. This may be an unusual feeling in mobile, middle-class North America, but I assure you it's quite common, and normal, in much of Europe and throughout the rest of the world. Belonging is important, and so are origins; Canada encourages national hyphenation—we're not a melting pot.

So let me tell you what Howdendyke village was like, and why it was destroyed, and what I feel about this microcosmic outrage of twentieth-century "progress" and "development." For Howdendyke is only an example of what is going on everywhere, the cleansing of the earth of real places, in the name of profit. If I burst into verse, it will be in an easy idiom. Poetry is one way of unburdening, of releasing and sharing the pain.

Howdendyke to the 1960s

Howdendyke was not one of those poster-pretty villages (most of which are full of commuters who don't belong). Its glory was its location in the swampy Humberhead region of Yorkshire, a district of many broad rivers (Aire, Derwent, Ouse, Trent, Humber), a Dutch-like flatness of deep straight drains, ancient farmland, windmills, ships, barges, the piling-up of cumulus on vast horizons, marvellous thunderstorms, that glorious, smelly, caking mud. The smell of rotting vegetation in mud, as in peat bog or mangrove swamp, takes me back instantly.

The village grew up at the entrance of a small creek feeding into the River Ouse. Up this creek was boated, in medieval times, the creamy limestone to build Howden Minster, a mile or so inland. A small port grew up thereafter, with a shipyard, a wharf for importing coal and timber, a ferry, and several small businesses. All this would have gone into decline with the coming of the railways, had not a West Yorkshire chemist created an agricultural fertilizer factory on the riverside in 1857. The village expanded around the factory, the whole surrounded by miles of hedged fields.

From 1857 until 1960, over a hundred years, the factory owners lived in the village, owned most of its houses, and provided most of its employment. A small shipyard (employing about fifteen) and a farm provided other jobs. The population stabilized at around two hundred or so by the early twentieth century, occupying about seventy houses. When I began to share the job of village postman at age eight (1951), the village boasted one pub, a village hall, one shop, and the post office where I lived. No one had cars or televisions; we lived locally and had local amusements (cricket and football teams, dances, whist drives, gardening, walking the fields, each other). A bus came on Wednesdays and Saturdays to take us to the town. Otherwise we walked or cycled.

Of course, all this would have changed as 1960s' affluence brought television (keeping people at home) and cars (taking them out of the village more often). But these factors would have changed the village, not destroyed it.

Annihilating a Place

Contingency is underrated. Things happen. The factory owner's only son was killed in the First World War. The daughter married, but had no children. Cousins weren't interested in taking on the plant. When the owners died in 1960, the factory was sold to a subsidiary of Imperial Chemical Industries, a huge conglomerate. "Rationalization" was the watchword, with product changes and company-owned housing being sold off or demolished.

Finding itself with too much vacant land "lying idle," the new company sold this off to Humberside Sea & Land Services (HS & L), another subsidiary of a large conglomerate. What was "Pol Pot Time" in Cambodia was Thatcher Time in Britain. Economic decisions were predicated on ideology and the bottom line. Despite the existence of the large port of Goole (20,000 people) five miles downstream, HS & L was determined to revive Howdendyke as a riverport, albeit on a much more massive scale. This fitted well with Thatcher's ideology, which was to "discipline" unionized workers such as the dock workers of Goole. Howdendyke was to be a nonunionized port, specializing (according to the official regional plan) in manufacturing industry based on imported raw materials. Jobs would be created in a depressed area.

A new factory sprang up on one side of the village. Mrs. Thatcher, amid great hoopla, came to open it. Shortly afterwards it went bust, and the site became not a manufacturing zone, as planned, but an import and distribution concern. On the other side of the village, HS & L purchased fields and built enormous, ugly warehouses. Suddenly, the small triangular village found itself almost completely ringed by industrial development where previously had been only fields.

Worse was to come. The heart of the village, the centre of the triangle, had in 1960 consisted of the original factory, an open field, and the square, which was the village centre with pub, hall, and post office. HS & L acquired part of the field and the square from the successor to the fertilizer company, and over a period of about twenty years the two companies began to demolish houses and institutions, as required, bit by bit.

How could this occur? Quite easily, and legally. Some houses needed attention. The fertilizer company refused to repair its houses for over a decade. Occupants complained. The local authority's Health and Housing Department asked the company to renovate, or face closure and condemnation orders. The company refused to comply, renters were moved to local authority public housing in nearby towns, and the village houses condemned as unfit for habitation. Whereupon the company knocked them down. When I asked the Health and Housing inspector why he'd chosen to inspect the pub just as the company was submitting a plan to demolish it and make the site a parking area, his flip reply was: "Life is full of coincidences."

In terms of planning applications, HS & L had a neat ploy. The company was granted planning permission to erect large warehouses. These then proved too big for the meagre capacity of the river jetties. Planning permission to expand the jetties being given, the company built them to a capacity which overloaded the warehouses. Whereupon warehouse enlargement was necessary, thus leading to jetty extensions and so on. More coincidences?

The planners, when confronted with the company's blatantly obvious contravention of the county structure plan, countered with the observation that Howdendyke had long been deemed "an exception to the plan." This was news to the inhabitants, who had never been consulted and who found out about the forthcoming destruction of their village only by newspaper reports or by waking up to find bulldozers at work.

Some local politicians were adamant that the village of

Howdendyke should be destroyed to create a new port and thus bring jobs to the district. The councillor in whose ward Howdendyke lay, however, refused me an interview. The HS & L manager proved hard to interview too, remarking that "it is in the nature of business to grow."

In my book *Planned to Death: The Annihilation of A Place Called Howdendyke* (Toronto: University of Toronto Press, 1989), I discuss in detail the possibility of conspiracy and the probability of opportunity-taking in a climate of like-mindedness among corporate executives, politicians, planners, and health and housing bureaucrats. These are middle-class people, far removed both spatially and mentally from the people of Howdendyke. They are more rootless too, and simply can't understand why anyone could refuse a nice new public housing unit in a town in favour of a run-down cottage, possibly without a bathroom or hot water, in what was rapidly becoming an industrial slum. In other words, these people have little sense of place and cannot appreciate place-loyalty, or do not wish to do so because such an appreciation would compromise their stern duty toward profit, jobs, and the grand plans in their heads.

Thus, just as Howdendyke found itself suddenly surrounded by industry in the 1970s, in the 1980s its heart was eaten out by the destruction of the village's central core. The seventy houses of 1960 had become, by 1997, only thirty-eight houses. And of these, only twenty-four were actually inhabited, fourteen being derelict or boarded up, awaiting demolition. My own house, the village post office, in the family for three generations, was pulled down in June 1997. I missed the demolition, but managed to get there in time to save a few eighteenth- and nineteenth-century bricks as mementos. These are individualistic, handmade bricks, some with fingermarks. They grace the table at which I write this piece.

Microcosm—Macrocosm

Take a trip into the future. Take the road to Howdendyke. Swing down the north end of the village street, where neat houses still face a looming and expanding factory. Halfway down the village you encounter a change: houses empty, many boarded up, a place run-down, nearly uninhabited, almost abandoned. Finally you reach the river bank and contemplate a high, concentration-camp fence beyond which lies an asphalt wasteland littered with mahogany logs and imported metal ingots. Ships loom above you. This black asphalt rectangle was once the village hub, with houses, village hall, post office, pub. All gone, and legally, to permit HS & L to transform a living village into a warehouse yard.

This is the world in microcosm. As you read this, almost two million Chinese are being evicted to make way for the reservoir behind the Three Gorges dam. Add to this all the dam-related evictions since 1945. Think of the dams now being erected in China, India, South-east Asia, South America. Then add to these all the millions of people moved, often against their will, to make way for urban renewal, airports, highways, port installations, wilderness national parks. Then more millions moved to "rationalize the settlement pattern" in Canada, Greenland, Norway, and, in both war and peace, the grand "villagization" schemes of Africa and Asia. Not to speak of home destruction via ethnic cleansing in Israel, South Africa, the former Yugoslavia, the former Soviet Union, Rwanda, and Burundi.

Everywhere loved landscapes and loved homes are blotted out, slaughtered, expunged for profit or ideology, or both. What we get instead are placeless blandscapes, malls, suburbia, "new towns," and "economic sites." The 25 million cross-border refugees of the world get some attention from the UN and other agencies; the greater number displaced unwillingly from their homes for ideology and profit get none. This is the world run by profiteers and technocrats, those with big plans. This is the world we've chosen as compliant "consumers." It will get worse.

My Feelings

What Howdendykers feel is expressed at length in *Planned to Death*. Here's how I feel about the murder of my village, the destruction of my home:

Councillor Brays about Howdendyke

Councillor Bray won't give an interview:
"I've nowt to say" he garbles down the 'phone.
He's had a lot to say in Boothferry Council
Meetings, about a village which he represents:
"I'd like to see it one big concrete slab.
It's such a mucky hole. And it means jobs."

Boothferry's a depressed area, or worse;
The call for "jobs" complies with Business Growth.
My village, say the planners, isn't bad,
It's just "in the wrong place," a lovely site
For berthing coasting vessels. It must pay the price
For half-a-dozen jobs. It's laughable
This argument, a village for ten jobs,
It's almost like a
Joke, unless, that is,
You are a Howdendyker.

I think, somehow, it's all to do with cash.
"Bray" is a Yorkshire word for "beat" or "smash."

Jobs

Workers with jobs come to destroy my place.
Cranes and bulldozers take these hovels down,
Crush up the ancient bricks. Women, old men
And kids look on in bafflement, as their known world
Collapses. It's rubble now, the Square, where
We had Bonfires, played Mischievous Night, and
Where our elders pubcrawled in one pub,
Shopped at the Post Office, danced the Hokey Cokey
In the hall. All rubble now, and better for it
Say the managers, to be asphalted over, a

"Hard standing" for a fleet of haulage trucks.

And now, what was irregular, and bright,
And three-dimensional, and full of life,
And wrong, shrivels to a harsh black flatness
Where stand oily shallows after rain.

My place is like a dying cut-down whale
With busy men dismantling, hacking, flensing.
Don't get me wrong, such work means jobs.
Jobs are a form of cleansing.

The Kubler-Ross Approach to Dying

Denial wasn't in the cards, so
I tried anger, it was only
Right to try to stop destruction,
Rage against unmitigated
Business murdering my village.
They were stronger, richer, harder.
Blandishments were tried, and threatening,
All of which distractions covered
Up the endless hopeless slither
Of the smothering of my village.

Now I've come to some acceptance

Yet I'll demonstrate their callous
Unforgiving work by witness,
Journalling the lies and truths a-
-bout the murder of my village:
The Kubler-Ross approach to dying.

Small Achievements, Big Lessons

Howdendyke had no local hero, although national and regional villains are much in evidence. By 2001 the village will probably have stabilized at around twenty houses (less than 30 per cent of its original size) and a pub (only a quarter of its original complement of public facilities). Stabilization will come only because the companies have secured (for now) all the waterfront land they need for new wharves, warehouses, and yards.

A variety of attempts were made to halt or mitigate the process of village destruction. Only minor achievements can be listed; the new pub is one of these. The publication of *Planned to Death* on two continents is another. The remaining villagers have used the book in protest meetings against further development; in its small way, it has been a catalyst. Further, the book may well have improved local self-esteem and shown Howdendykers that they are not forgotten (at the very least, it's a memorial volume). A number of Howdendykers have appreciated the opportunity given by the book for them to tell their stories; this provides both a counter to official propaganda and some measure of psychological release. This release has certainly been of benefit to me, being part of a major creative effort which has helped to assuage my grief (Freud calls this "abreaction," I call it "writing it out").

The book has also led to the public exposure of the perpetrators of village destruction, and demonstrates the underhanded and unfeeling way in which they went about it. This has not led to any apologies (powerful people find it hard to apologize; witness the Japanese over their war atrocities). But a single case of personal benefit has made the writing of the book worthwhile. I believe it had at least some role in causing one of the companies to finally renovate one of its remaining company cottages, providing a widow in her seventies, for the first time, with a hot-water system and a bathroom. It's hard to believe that anyone could be without these amenities in the 1990s. Vera, however, although very pleased with these new facilities (you should have seen her smile!), would not have voluntarily left her cottage for a "better" place elsewhere. She sums up the whole situation in her remarks: "This is my home. We were happy here. I'm happy here. All my memories are here." This is the place-loyalty, the material basis of identity and security, that the destroyers cannot (or rather, will not) understand.

Vera died in 1998, leaving only two occupants in one cottage in a nine-unit, company-owned row. Once these occupants die, or are relocated because of age or illness to a "home" ("long-term care facility" nowadays), this whole row of excellent, well-built cottages will be bulldozed. I suppose we should be grateful that these last occupants have not already been forced out. But perhaps the company doesn't need the land yet.

Tiny achievements, I agree, but big lessons. What Howdendyke has taught me is that the village is a microcosm of a world-wide phenomenon. Being an academic, I've developed a sort of theory. Briefly, it states that place-annihilation is frequent, widespread, and common to all phases of recorded history. It often involves forcible or coerced eviction. This is usually justified by mantras such as "in the national interest," "rationalization," "economic necessity," and "progress." Soft-soaping euphemisms are commonly employed: relocation, displacement, resettlement, villagization, urban renewal (the latter is an example of the Big Lie). Legislation may be enacted, from the resettlement schemes of Canada, Greenland, and Norway to the Group Areas Act of apartheid South Africa. Both material (profit) and psychological ("we implemented this wonderful project") benefits accrue to the perpetrators, usually business and/or government. In contrast, many oustees receive little or no compensation (ask the Indians turned out of their homes for the Narmada dams). Benefits accrue nationally and regionally (a new dam or airport, for example) whereas disbenefits occur locally ("the comfort of the few must be sacrificed for the good of the many"). Among the evicted, a grief syndrome is quite common; some elderly evictees die prematurely. Resistance is difficult; the perpetrators hold all the cards, command all the bulldozers. Information is withheld. Above all, the perpetrators are powerful, articulate, middle-class people, whereas the evictees are very often working-class people, inner-city dwellers, visible minorities, scattered rural folk, or Aboriginal peoples. Such people may not be articulate, do not know the law, cannot command the services of lawyers and accountants, and find the prospect of opposing "them" quite daunting. And, let's face it, the many middle-class beneficiaries of eviction-causing projects are likely to consider such groups to be of no account.

So what use is theory anyway? Well, before you can right a wrong you need to be able to recognize it and speak articulately about it. The phenomenon has to have a name. Connections between apparently isolated incidents must be made. At the beginning of the twentieth century, few people could conceptualize "refugee," "genocide" or "ecocatastrophe." These terms now have their place in international discussions. Agencies, official (UN) and unofficial (NGOs), have been set up to deal with these problems. We now have Greenpeace, earth summits, and global emission standards.

My modest proposal, then, is that we recognize place-annihilation as a major, world-wide phenomenon of forcible or coerced eviction that involves probably at least as many people as are currently registered as international refugees. Evictees are usually internal refugees, and thus not easily recognized as an international concern. But they could certainly become so, once the connection is made between the victims of dams in India, China, and Brazil and the victims of new airports, dams, "urban renewal," and parks in the industrial world. If a better name than place-annihilation is required, let's try the neologisms of topocide (the destruction of place, an "objective" phenomenon) and/or domicide (the destruction of home, a subjective or "felt" phenomenon). Both of these may lead to memoricide, the forgetting that any such place ever existed (a major war goal of the Bosnian Serbs vis-à-vis Bosnian Muslims).

More generally still, we need new ways to think about "progress" and whether what capitalists call progress is ultimately for anyone's good, or for the earth's (it's very satisfying since 1991 to be able to reverse the old American dictum and say: "If you like capitalism so much, why don't you go to Russia?"). And we need to remember that while NIMBY (not in my back yard) isn't always justified, NSBOTOMY (not smack-bang on top of my yard) is a valid position.

Only the Beginning

> Houses live and die; there is a time for building . . .
> And a time for the wind to break the loosened pane . . .
>
> T. S. Eliot

Don't believe Eliot. Ultimately, he's right, but when your own home is threatened it is better to take Dylan Thomas's advice: "Do not go gentle . . ."

For it's not the end, it's only the beginning. Triumphalist global capitalism blankets the world, steadily homogenizing, Disneyfying, and reducing authenticity. As you read this, distinctive places are being slaughtered and deleted from the map. When we all live in placeless suburbias and apartments, place-loyalty will die, to be re-placed by loyalty to brand-names and franchised football teams. Countries, of course, will be long gone, replaced by economic blocs. The future, for the northern hemisphere at least, is a Brave New World inside a 1984. None of this is a problem, says money-squandering NASA, for when we've fucked up the earth we (only some of us, naturally) can escape to the delights of the Moon, or Mars (another giant step for e. e. cummings's "busy monster, manunkind").

If the above scenario appals, what can one do? Several things have worked for me. They may work for you, too. First, become aware of how the world operates biologically, economically, geographically, politically. Read a newspaper that's not owned by a wealthy individual or corporation. Try the alternative press. Peruse Edward Abbey, Eric Hobsbawm, Christopher Alexander. Watch Suzuki. Second, be alert to unwanted environmental change in wilderness, countryside, or city. Third, oppose it. Band together as citizens against—. Fourth, spread the word about alternatives: nature-caring, city-humanizing, right-living citizens for—. Fifth, consider a life of cooperation, rather than competition. Sixth, think laterally, be imaginative; don't just accept what corporations, bureaucrats, or politicians want to give you; ask what's in it for them. Seventh, above all don't think of yourself as a "consumer." To be merely a consumer is to become Coleridge's "nightmare death in life." Make something: makers are poets. Eighth, adopt a space or place as your "field of care." If you own it, so much the better. A suburban front lawn, for instance, is a dull, expensive, idiotic way of conforming with set-back regulations. Just tear it out and replace it with a bamboo forest, a potato field, a Japanese garden, or something of your own devising. Be a suburban guerrilla. Ninth: well, you get the idea. Time to stop preaching.

J. DOUGLAS PORTEOUS

And if, despite your efforts, your place has gone, it's a good idea to re-place yourself. It takes time, as I've discovered as an immigrant to Canada. What has helped me is an active involvement in the shaping of a number of small environments, ranging from a 0.1-acre inner city backyard in Victoria, British Columbia, to a forty-six-acre farm on nearby Saturna Island. These enjoyable and root-making landscape design and maintenance projects have varied from the planting of new trees (city) to the removal of trees and the development of a meadow (countryside). The tools I favour are scythe, long-handled snips, and a Nicaraguan machete (with a few whacks the latter will take down a fifteen-foot softwood sapling). Chainsaw and brushcutter come out only briefly. The ultimate result is a series of pleasant landscapes in which (although I own only one of them) I have some psychic investment and connection with both the earth and some of its people.

On my own small property, I'm helping to restore the land to what is as near as possible its natural state (second-growth dry Douglas fir biome). Broom and other rampant exotics are eradicated, although I leave a few exotic ferals such as foxglove and woolly mullein. Salal (tasty berries, gorgeous leaves, seventy cents a stalk in the city) smothers the former owner's daffodils. Oregon grape's my holly. Native flowering red currant brings the hummingbirds back every March. A few feral daisies emerge from the local grasses, but I prefer the native spotted coral root orchid that grows in the duff below the trees. Tall Douglas fir and cedar sway a hundred feet above. Arbutus sheds bark and leaves about me. My shack's painted in arbutus bark colours, dark brown, orange, deep, rich oxblood red. The shack is like a cave, cool in the hottest summer, looking out into the forest with glimpses of ocean beyond (if I'd cut the trees, I'd have "a view"). This is my field of care; I love it.

The Environment of Work

Richard Pickard

THREE GENERATIONS OF MEN STAND TOGETHER. HANDS STUFFED in front pockets of pants, or arms crossed high across chests. The men make the same facial gestures, two of them looking down and nodding soberly as the other talks. Then, as the speaker finishes, the listeners look up with a smile, a shake of the head, or a semi-incredulous grimace. Chances are these men are looking at something in the garden, or in the barn. Or in the bush.

When I was growing up I frequently stood this way with my father and grandfather, three Pickard men, in a sense the same man at three different ages and the products of three different eras. My grandfather rarely leaves his farm, so these situations would usually occur while we were looking at some productive portion of his land. We would seem to be consulting each other, but we would always know the same answers to the same questions. A decision would be made, and we would either move on to something else—the pheasants maybe, or this year's calf, or a tree ready to come down across the road—or we would get back to work. When my grandparents visited my parents, we three men would bring in one or more loads of firewood from the hill across the valley, and there would be several such moments of collective thought: perhaps admiring a view or a particularly good fall by my dad, maybe gauging the effort involved in bringing some lengths of timber back up the slope to the road, or figuring how better to stack wood in the back of the truck.

Today when we stand together, the intimacy of work is missing. We assemble at reunions, birthday parties, anniversaries—the "special occasions" whose ordinariness belies their names and yet whose specialness robs us of more intimate points of contact. My father and grandfather share the same connections even when they are not standing before a fallen tree or a fattening steer, but I enter their world as almost a foreigner. We share the stance, the gestures, but the meaning of those gestures has changed. Even our silence has changed; once it was a feeling of fellowship, now it feels more like the mental discomfort of separation.

The loss I feel most strongly is the loss of the world I once co-inhabited through work with my father and grandfather. As David Abram says in *The Spell of the Sensuous* (New York: Vintage-Random House, 1996), living with technology—out of contact with the natural world—is a precarious situation. And I feel this precariousness in a very personal way, because at my workplace my body, written on by the same genetic code that marks the bodies of my father and grandfather, occupies a cubicle eight feet wide and fourteen feet long—so unlike the large lumber mill where my father works and the virtually unlimited outdoor landscape of my grandfather's farm and region (now increasingly limited by the environmental rules and regulations that I work on).

My grandfather has spent his life, since returning from the Second World War, in the woods as a logger and on the land as a subsistence farmer. My father grew up on several farms on southern Vancouver Island, and has worked for most of his adult life in the forest industry, first planting trees and as a general labourer, then in a mill as a grader. I'm completing a PhD in English on literature and the environment, and I'm working as a policy analyst on contract with the British Columbia Ministry of Environment. Our working lives, once so similar, now differ vastly; at least mine differs from theirs, and that is made even clearer by the contrasting professional relationship I have with nature.

Participation

One of my clearest memories of growing up is the one chance I had to help exercise my grandfather's cougar hounds. We drove several miles out along a dirt road west of Errington to the power line, where there was a wide strip of scrubby clearing. The strip was littered with trunks of trees that had been cut to protect the lines, and was filling in with brush and small trees. Once we got there, my uncle Tom and I took turns playing coon for the hounds.

My grandfather had tied to a length of rope the skin of one of the many raccoons he had trapped or shot—their reward for stalking his chickens. He would give either Tom or me a head-start of a few minutes, and we'd take off running with the coonskin dragging behind us while Granddad held back the hounds. After fifteen minutes or so he'd release them, and the chase would be on. Once they got close you had to throw the lure up into a tree or on top of a brush pile they couldn't climb, because you didn't want to waste a pelt. (Nor did you want the hounds tearing you to bits as they tried to get at the bait.) Throwing it was an admission of defeat, but it was also an acknowledgement of work well done on their part and yours.

I remember struggling up a steep sand cutbank above the road. Dust in my throat and nose from my hands and feet skidding as I laboured upward; lungs aching from the effort of the climb after ten or fifteen minutes of hard running through difficult terrain; the sun hot on my bare, damp, dust-streaked back; sweat stinging the raw skin where the rope had chafed across my wrist in rhythm with my strides. The hounds appeared around a corner of the road, baying loudly, and I reluctantly hurled the pelt into a fir tree's branches. I didn't want this moment to be over, despite, or perhaps because of, the heat, the effort, the sense of hard work achieved.

I have rarely felt as alive as I did then.

Even though it was just a good way to exercise the hounds, I see it now as a pivotal moment in my understanding of my grandfather and his life. It was then that I realized bodily the possibilities and meaning of a life spent working in nature. The boundaries of self and other have never been so clear and at the same time so irrelevant as they were on that cutbank. The rope and the coonskin, entirely separate from my body, were in a sense a part of my body that kept the hounds pursuing me. They chased me, following the path I traced for them (and tried to obscure from them), and yet they disregarded me entirely once I threw the coonskin into the branches. I was taking advantage of the hounds' reliance on their senses, but I was racing them, testing them physically, and finding them more able than I.

I used to think that the bodily reality of my grandfather's labour—written in the calluses of his knuckles, the texture of his forehead, the slight stoop of an arthritic spine—represented a lack of separation of work from life, or of his life from the nature in which he has worked for so long. He was for me a part of nature, more like a force of nature than just another person. My time as the hounds' quarry revealed additional complexity to a life like his, but I still didn't understand the implications of living such a life, or what it would mean for me to live the kind of life that I was going to start leading in a few years.

Pain

My earliest memories are of physical pain: my grandparents' tom turkey knocking me down when I was three; falling from a parked pickup truck into a gravel driveway at four and getting twelve stitches in my forehead; at five getting glass in my thumb from breaking the bulb of a heat lamp I'd been told not to play with. Many of my strongest memories since then have been of pain as well, as I loved sports but was too small for the success I might otherwise have enjoyed; in high school I was usually several inches shorter and twenty or more pounds lighter than my opposite number in rugby and basketball, so pain was a normal part of the game.

I think now that maybe I sought out pain as a way of anchoring myself in the world. My father worked in the mill while I was in high school, and my grandfather worked the farm, but I had a different path before me. My grades were good enough that I was sent to boarding school in the big city, in Victoria, and it had been clear even before that time that I was not intended for physical labour. Not that I wasn't capable of it, but my family hoped I would be able to rise above the purely physical. I worked on the farms of our neighbours, and helped with the chores on our own place (milking the goats, gathering eggs, slaughtering chickens, bringing loads of firewood from the hill), but this was not to be my working life. These jobs were only temporary. This was not to be my way of relating to the world on a permanent basis.

Injuries, athletic and otherwise, brought me pain, and pain was also a visible part of my father's life at the mill and of my grandfather's on the farm. School provided me with no such affirmation of reality. For a while my extracurricular farm work and sporting injuries helped maintain a link with my father and grandfather; my injuries were a kind of language they understood and admired intuitively, instinctively. I needed this pain and the relationship it brought to make sense out of my world, a world that was rapidly becoming only mine. It wasn't theirs. They did not, could not, enter my world of boarding school, cramped writing, and a gradual divorce from what lay directly outside my window.

Their life and work, in and with nature, was marked indelibly on and under their skin. The wrinkles on my grandfather's skin showed me how much time he spent outdoors in all kinds of weather. The ring of scar tissue on my father's thumb reminded me (and no doubt reminded him at least as clearly) of the day he nearly cut it off with an axe. The signs that spoke of their past, present, and future lives are visible on their bodies, and I was and am envious. I cannot help feeling that their lives are more real than mine.

Mystery

I was never given the opportunity to understand the lumber mill where my father works, never initiated into its mysteries. Because of this I probably place too much emphasis on my father's workplace, but it is an emphasis I seem unable to resist.

My father and I would go to the mill occasionally, such as to fill our one-hundred-gallon tank with water when our regular water supply froze or dried up (depending upon the season). We would drive past the mill when we would go camping in a particular direction from home, or when we drove to Silver Spray Falls. And when we went fishing in Adams Lake we launched our boat near the mill and caught our largest fish near the logbooms. But I never went inside, just to see it, until a visit that my then-fiancée made with me to my parents. I was surprised when Dad offered to take us (her, really) to see the mill. She was a city girl in some senses and she immediately agreed, knowing it would be an interesting experience. It shocked her that this would also be my first visit to my father's workplace—at least to see the inner workings of the mill, and my father's working life, in any detail.

We wore hardhats and earplugs as we walked through every building of the production line, following the same path that a log did. Dad and my fiancée walked together as he shouted explanations in her ear over the din of machinery, she passing it on to me whenever she could do so. I was virtually left out of my first and so far only tour of the lumber mill. I've no doubt he left me out unintentionally, in a way, but why? And why didn't he take me through the mill earlier?

The first answer is that he wanted to make sure I wasn't seduced by the easy lure of large machinery and raw technological power, as boys frequently are. Mom has often said that he specifically hoped I wouldn't work there, as he didn't want me to have the same kind of working life he did. Keeping me away from his workplace might keep me from making the choice to follow my father that so many sons have made over the years. It is sometimes an easy choice, sometimes a difficult one, but it is almost always available. My father didn't want it available to me.

But maybe he thought I would just know, would just understand about life at the mill. He may have thought I would learn by osmosis, as he had about his father's work on the family farm. The great difference of course is that Dad actually worked on the farm, whereas I only heard about the mill over dinner (and usually only about the men he worked with, No Go and Chit-Chat and J.R. and so on). He assumed a daily connection that, had it ever existed, he helped to sever by sending me to boarding school and thereby encouraged me to imagine for myself only a world outside of physical labour.

Working in the Present

My grandfather still works on the farm, though he has now sold most of it to his youngest son; my uncle has built a house for himself and his family where the big chicken coop once stood. In recent years Granddad has survived a cancer scare and radiation therapy, some of the technologies about which I've been educated entering his very body. Our connection is not as deep as it was, in spite of his encounters with technology, for we still occupy different worlds. Just as I drop in on his, and admire the chickens, the fences, the twin lambs, he has had to learn to admire and respect the technology that has freed him from this particular threat of death. We cannot discuss the ways in which we enter each other's worlds, and neither of us feel comfortable there, but that's how we can spend time together. Sometimes that time means everything. And sometimes it means nothing. Occasionally a visit to his world will rejuvenate my own, just as his trips to Victoria's cancer clinic have extended his life. But on other visits, I return to my world disgruntled, angry, sure of my uselessness. My world then feels false and worthless.

Dad is trying to move out of the lumber mill and become a full-time photographer, but he's not able to leave the physicality out of his work. He takes pictures of nature and landscapes, and shows them in slide-shows that he narrates in terms of the physical exertion he put into capturing the images we see so effortlessly. He continues to work at the mill and is training for a new job there, but the photography is really the centre of his life now (especially the hiking that gains him access to the privileged wildernesses above the treeline). His sales of pictures still won't allow him to retire from the mill, but they subsidize his quasi-environmentalist pursuits.

And me? For the past year I have had two occupations—and I don't inhabit the physical world of my father and grandfather in either one. I expect to receive a doctorate in English this summer (specializing in eighteenth-century poetry about nature), and for the past year I've spent evenings and weekends working toward that goal. At the same time, I've been working as a policy analyst and technical writer on contract with the British Columbia Ministry of Environment, Lands, and Parks. My occupations are in many ways not that far from the land; both require me to reimagine the physical world, to rethink the way people might/should/did respond to their surroundings.

But I sit with pen in hand, or fingers poised over keyboard, and the artificial light of my home or office buzzes in the background. I discuss the best way to approach poachers, or I read a long georgic poem about sheep. How can this be my work? How can this be real? How can my work be read by me? By others? By my father and grandfather? And how does this kind of work rewrite the genetic and physical characteristics that I share with my forebears?

In my scholarship I try to reimagine ecological ideas and to question environmentalism's background in Romantic literature, especially

Wordsworth's poetry. Our understanding of Romanticism has solidified the binary that hamstrings postmodern environmentalism (nature is either empty of humans, or it is ruined). My job academically is to question both the binary and the neoromantic impulses that sustain the binary's life. I try to bring ideas of work back into the equation, to think of a world in which work is part of a healthy ecology and a sign of environmental promise. I read long poems, georgics, that set out what eighteenth-century poets saw as the best way to address nature through work (on gardens, in orchards, with flocks of sheep, and so on), and I imagine the kind of world that the writers might have hoped would come from people taking their advice.

In my work for the Ministry of Environment I write policies and procedures for the Conservation Officers Service, on management of problem wildlife and high-risk vehicle stops and similar topics, so I try to ensure the same possibility of a healthy ecology in the future. I interpret legislation and regulations, negotiate the terms of agreements with other agencies, and consult with staff in local offices across the province to ensure that (since I'm writing on their behalf) I have the correct information from them about their needs.

These documents are written, in my simultaneous careers, in a human-made environment thoroughly removed from the reality of conservancy and hunting. I work far from the possibility of that moment of aliveness I felt in throwing the pelt into the fir's branches, tasting salt and fear and exhilaration and connection to other generations and to the land. My father and grandfather are proud of the work and life that

I now live, yet I ponder their lives instead, and compare mine unfavourably to theirs. I don't think any of us expected that through professional and scholarly success I would feel I had lost the earth.

Imagining the Future

I don't mean to get maudlin about all this, and I'm grateful for the opportunities that I've been given. I get along with my father and grandfather quite well, though we don't talk about much when we see each other or when we speak on the phone. They're interested in hearing what I'm doing at work or at school, and appreciate any help I can give them when we visit.

It's just that they live in a world I can no longer occupy, even for a short time. I can stack wood, or pick eggs, or spend a day hoisting bales of hay onto a trailer, but it's not my world. It's theirs. We meet in a kind of parallel universe, neither my world nor theirs, a universe I find myself increasingly drawn to think about in my academic work. Industry and environmentalism are in constant struggle, especially in British Columbia, but there are no opportunities for their representatives to speak to each other, to communicate through common language. We Pickard men seem to be trying to find that place for ourselves in our own lives. We are seeking to avoid being pressed into silence by differences because we recognize and live through the similarities that bind us: not just work and the environment, but the genetics visible in our rising hairlines and our bony shoulders.

The future? My grandfather will continue to work his Vancouver

Island farm until he can no longer do so, and with luck he will be able to remain on the farm after his work is done to watch and help his son and grandsons maintain the place. My father and I will continue to visit Granddad and will continue to share in his knowledge of the land as well as of the plants and animals he raises. A hundred miles from home is a long way for Granddad, because that is about the limit of his deep knowledge; Vancouver Island for him stretches from Port Alberni through Parksville and Nanaimo to Duncan. Victoria is the site of his cancer treatments and periodic checkups, but that city is not part of his island.

Victoria is, however, where I live and work. The roots of my life are in Parksville, and in the Shuswap area of interior British Columbia where my parents live. My academic work requires the assistance of professors in Edmonton, Alberta, and builds on criticism written by people living in the United States, Europe, and Australia. My professional activity gives words to the experiences of people working in Atlin, Dease Lake, Fort St. John, Keremeos, offices in places all around British Columbia—places I've never been. It is only the first-generation city-dweller who has such distant roots, because the city provided none for me when I arrived.

My father will continue to work at Adams Lake Lumber, part of the Interfor group of mills, until he can afford to retire. When he does retire it will be to spend as much time as he can in work even more physically taxing, though more varied. The persistent ache in his left forearm and left knee from flipping boards as he grades them will give way to more generalized pain from climbing steep slopes and skidding down loose scree, packing sixty or so pounds of camera gear. We will continue to wonder about each other's lives and work, and will try to talk about it all without putting too much pressure on the moment of contact.

It is work, finally, that distinguishes each of us from the others, but it is also through work that we can define ourselves. Work gives us the frame on which to hang our similarities and our differences. Even more specifically, it is the work-world we live in and the imperfect understanding of our own and the other's environment that provides the intellectual ground on which we can meet. We converge, finally, not through my grandfather's continuous farm improvements that we admire, not through my father's slides of places where my grandfather and I have never been and may never visit, not through the abstractions I deal in and create in my professional and academic worlds. We meet through work, through knowledge of the daily labour it takes to learn a place, to learn our place, intimately.

We work not just to gain a living, but to earn—and keep—our lives.

Fireweeds, Blue Roses, and Bioethics
Where are We Going so Fast?

Iain E. P. Taylor

AS A CHILD IN ENGLAND, I LEARNED THAT HUMAN ACTIVITIES, such as war and smog, were bad for me. The members of my extended family were all farmers or gardeners. I picked wild flowers and occasionally dug up a plant to take home to my garden. I collected frog spawn and birds' eggs, and chased field mice on bombsites. I sometimes wondered if what I did was bad for Nature, but it seemed silly; I only took a little bit and surely the plants and animals would always be there.

I don't remember life without plants, in the town park or the botanical garden. Everyone I knew was curious and excited about plants. These people were eager students and teachers and I soon learned to look for interesting plants wherever I went. Although my professional research "jollies" were to come from plant physiology and physics, I have never been released from an inner desire, almost a sense of duty, to proselytize for plants. My scientific career took me into editing and now I aspire to be a scientific ethicist. I seem to have come full circle. I still worry that what we may do to plants is bad for Nature, but

I now have a wider sense of the world and the need for a strong environmental ethic. Will applications of plant biotechnology threaten the environment? Is sustainability really possible? Does anyone have a right to claim ownership of Nature? I drive long hours in an air-polluting car to a rural retreat where my neighbours are pristine lakes, old-growth sub-alpine forests, wilderness, and Aboriginal peoples, as well as clear-cuts and property developers waiting for the next wave of recreational property owners. I like to think that I am a responsible steward. I know that I must nurture Nature and avoid "control freak" instincts to transplant my urban desires for order and tidiness. If I mess too much with the plants, if I do not consider my offshoots, "they'll never receive any blessing from" Nature.

Messing with Nature could be Hazardous to Your Health

I don't know when humans first messed with Nature. The argument between astronomy and botany for bragging rights as the oldest science may never be resolved. However, throughout human history societies have had particular respect for individuals who invoke the powers of plants for medical uses, in religious and cultural rites, or to explain the significance of celestial events. Certainly, humans have been messing with plants for hundreds of thousands of years; we include our modern endeavours in disciplines such as agriculture, forestry, pharmacy, and most recently biotechnology.

At the beginning of the twenty-first century, there is much controversy about the intensity of agriculture and the emerging potential of genetic engineering. Scientists have learned to synthesize new genes, to transfer genes between organisms of the same species, and to introduce genes from other species, even from other kingdoms. The benefits, we are told, are there for the good of humankind. To object or suggest caution can lead to castigation for denying humanity access to benefits that are claimed to be almost limitless, and involve trivial risks or no risks at all.

Yet we would be wise to consider humanity's history of messing about with Nature before we become irreversibly hitched to this latest scientific wonder solution. The written record is only recent, but major domestications, such as those that have led to the modern cultivars of crop plants, have had enormous positive and negative effects on humanity. The current worldwide population explosion demands that we become much more efficient in our use and distribution of Nature's bounty if we are not to suffer more massive starvation than is occurring in many parts of the world. We stand on the threshold of a new technology, one that may have greater impact than any that has gone before. We will do well to remember that the relatively low technology of plant breeding that brought us the food benefits of rice, potato, and corn also gave us the poorly predicted social dilemmas of tobacco and coca. The full consequences of scientific advance, in terms of sociological impacts, have rarely been accurately predicted.

Humanity had messed about with a lot of plants before 1938, the year I was born. I don't think that 1938 was a particularly inauspicious year, but changes in both the natural and agricultural world seem to have occurred at an unprecedented, dare I say uncontrolled, rate in the last sixty years. No matter how one perceives these changes, it is clear that botanical science is the foundation of much of our current cascading technological progress in agriculture, forestry, pharmacy, and other plant-related technologies.

In 1938, botany was in the midst of the age of cytogenetics, the study of chromosomes. Although human eugenics was in disrepute because of its association with the idea of creating a super race, selective plant breeding (eugenics) for disease resistance was the driving force of what would become modern plant pathology. The first electron microscope was a reality, albeit a cumbersome gadget. Plant collectors from all over the world were sending a seemingly endless supply of new and exotic plant specimens to the great herbaria and botanical gardens such as Leiden, Kew, Berlin, New York, and Kirstenbosch. One or two years of botanical study were part of the required curriculum in almost all medical, pharmacy, and veterinary schools. The study of plant hormones was in its infancy. We had little appreciation of the enormous advances of that research, both to the understanding of plant growth and for the design of synthetic herbicides.

Where are the Wild Flowers?

I only came to understand some of the serious consequences for plants arising from human activity, such as war and production of smog, decades after my childhood. The bombs had caused destruction, first mechanical then radioactive, on a scale never before imagined. The battlefields and bombed sites were left derelict, but my child's eyes saw the dereliction softened, even brightened, by fireweed and other opportunistic plants. Little wonder that I thought of Nature as supremely resilient. One serious negative effect of the Second World War was that we rarely found the flowers that my grandmother and other relations told me had grown in the woods and hedgerows when they were young—the primroses, bluebells, wild daffodils, and orchids. There used to be primroses in the woods of the Duke of Westminster's estate, near Chester, where I grew up, but somehow I could never find them. Of course, we were trespassing and shouldn't have been there to look in the first place.

All my family, old and young alike, knew about plants and had gardens where they grew flowers, fruits, and vegetables for the house and even to take to market. Almost every weekend was an opportunity to ride my tricycle in the country lanes, or to take a bus or a train on the way for a walk in the country. We children never really understood the war, even though few of us had resident Dads and there were always soldiers around. Small boys were expected to give up their seats on the bus to older people, and it seemed that finding a seat on a full bus was the signal for a soldier to get on at the very next stop. In spite of the uncertainty of travel, I looked forward to our regular Sunday walk and enthusiastically picked the flowers and pleaded to be allowed to take "just one or two" plants home to my garden. So did everyone else. It was very rare to find primroses, cowslips, or bluebells within thirty miles of most large British cities. We were a double threat. We dug up the plants, but then we forgot to replant them in our urban gardens. We were part of what proved to be a wave of massive environmental degradation.

Someone always claimed to know where we found the lady slippers last year or would recall a particular field that used to be covered in Easter lilies (wild daffodils). But somehow they were never there when I went walking. However, we small children were not deterred. We picked the ubiquitous dandelions—there seem to be so many more today—and made daisy chains. We collected frog's eggs and the occasional newt from marl pits that were in every Cheshire field, and took them home to face certain death by neglect in a jam jar. We fished for roach with a penny fishhook baited by a spitball of stale bread, but we did not realize why older children from the village actually caught big fish. In spite of the setbacks, it all seems so idyllic in retrospect.

The 1950s and 1960s were momentous times for systematic botany in the United Kingdom of my youth. The scientists who had been drafted to "the war effort" returned to their research with new vigour. Hooker's *Student's Flora of the British Isles* (London: Macmillan & Co., 1870), which had served as the benchmark botanical resource since its publication but required much knowledge to use, was supplanted on the bookshelves of amateur and professional alike by *Flora of British Isles* (Cambridge: Cambridge University, 1952), authored by Clapham, Tutin, and Warburg. Armed with CTW, as we knew it, plus the volumes of exquisite drawings of every flowering plant in Britain published from the Royal Botanic Gardens at Kew and the Reverend Keble Martin's magnificent water-colour illustrations in his best-selling coffeetable book *The Concise British Flora in Colour* (London: George Rainbird Ltd., 1952), any student who was interested in plants was, as we said in Liverpool, "all made up." Even teenagers had a good chance of correctly identifying plants collected on a country walk.

By the mid-1950s the British government had started building freeways and the steam trains were being replaced by diesels. These two seemingly unrelated events had enormous impact on the British countryside and its flora. The authorities excluded pedestrians and grazing animals from the freeways. The railway lines had always been fenced, but the hot ashes from the steam locomotives caused grass fires along the embankments—especially during the summer. These and the controlled-burning programs to reduce accidental fires certainly cut the floral diversity along otherwise protected areas. The diesel locomotives made fumes but did not spew ashes; hence there were few if any fires and the boulevards and banks were not subject to flower picking and grazing by farm animals. The result of these changes in road and rail was a system of strip nature reserves, which in a relatively few years began to show the floral diversity that had been such a clear part of my parents' reminiscences. The primroses and the bluebells returned in spring, the cowslips and mayflowers were blooming in May, and England's green and pleasant land was retinted with the colours of old. There was even a short time when we humans seemed to have learned to reduce our inappropriate messing with plants.

The Path to a Profession

I didn't start to study biology in school until 1953, when I was fifteen. I wanted to learn biology, but it was not an Ordinary-level exam subject in my school and this lazy teenager jumped at the chance to reduce his study load. Most of my peers wanted to be doctors. So did I until I discovered that you had to pass physics. The biology teacher, Mrs. Olive James, insisted that we study advanced-level botany and zoology separately. So, with chemistry, which I really did enjoy, I had my required three subjects and I had shaken the bonds of physics forever. Or so I thought.

My path to an honours degree in botany at the University of Liverpool was deliberately chosen as the line of least resistance. The professors certainly did their part, but the obligatory field excursions after first, second, and third year courses were the critical events for me. After first year, we spent a week studying in the rolling South Downs near Box Hill (of *Pickwick Papers* fame). After second year, it was the limestone clints and grikes of the Yorkshire Pennines at Malham Tarn. The highlight of third year was a two-week visit to the University of Liverpool field station at Port Erin, Isle of Man, where we studied marine biology and the biology of polluted waters, specifically the effluent from the brewery at Port St. Mary. The instructors were internationally known experts and were the catalysts who provided the seminal experiences that cemented my personal and professional lives together. The fact that each field excursion was blessed with sunny weather was an unexpected bonus. Most of us were not destined to become ecologists or systematic biologists, but the seeds of a lifelong commitment to biology as the study of whole organisms were sown on those trips. Occasional reunions and reminiscences still include recall of the scientific and social experiences that were such an integral part of the collegiality that fifty young people enjoyed in the three or four years of shared university education.

Pesticides

Alas, the "wonders" of pesticides and weed killers were also children of the 1940s, 1950s, and 1960s. Farmers who had brought every possible acre into wartime food production now used the new chemical fertilizers and pesticides to obtain greater and more consistent yield from their fields. Seemingly space-wasting hedgerows, some of which were many hundreds of years old, were torn out to increase productive acreage. Few realized that the price of this increased agricultural efficiency included the systematic destruction of the floral refugia that were the species banks for floral diversity. Outdoor workers and campers appreciated the pesticides because they reduced the irritating midges and gnats that troubled them as they worked the farms and enjoyed recreation in the Scottish Highlands or the mountains of Northern England and Wales. However, the selective herbicide sprays did not always land on the weeds among the crops and, by the early 1960s, some of our old wildflower haunts were once again threatened. Frankly, even the most ardent field botanists were not much aware of the effects of synthetic herbicide use.

Pesticides are not unnatural substances. Many plants, such as the pines and asters, thrive because they contain noxious substances that deter grazing animals or disease-causing microbes. Some of the chemicals may cause harm to humans: a walk through dense forest undergrowth in temperate rain forests such as those on the west coast of North America may lead to a painful encounter with devil's club, stinging nettles, or, for an unlucky few, a tiny liverwort that can cause a severe allergic reaction. However, the pesticides developed for agricultural use in the 1940s through 1960s were assessed for their affects on the pest (weed or insect); ill-effects on humans were rarely considered seriously. The publication of Rachel Carson's *Silent Spring* (Boston: Houghton Mifflin Company, 1962) was a bombshell for many, although others, including some plant scientists, saw its warnings as scaremongering. Fortunately, some of the more obvious animal destruction proved partly recoverable. The majestic eagles fly again; the peregrine falcons have found exciting new habitat on the cliffs of our cities' high-rise buildings. The plants may not have fared so well—whoever saw placard-carrying demonstrators calling for us to save the plants? The destruction of weedy plants by herbicides has given us fields of high-yield crops, but we now know that the residues have severely reduced populations of microscopic soil organisms and have damaged soil texture. In temperate regions, crop yield may be sustainable using either chemical or organic farming, but the record shows that botanical diversity is being drastically reduced. The International Union for the Conservation of Nature Red List of Threatened Plants (IUCN, Gland,

Switzerland, and Cambridge, UK) reports that 12.5 per cent (34,000 species) of the world's higher plant flora is endangered, in some cases almost to the point of extinction. Agricultural practices have been major contributors to these losses.

The pesticides that kill the insects do not select the pests from the natural pollinators. Those plants that rely on very specific insects, such as the forage crop alfalfa, will not produce much seed unless their specific pollinator is available. The "rediscovery" of natural pesticides is certainly a step in the right direction, but we must all learn that biological control rather than eradication is probably the only attainable objective. Clearly, Nature has never been able to make eradication work. Humans should look to Nature more frequently to be reminded of that wisdom.

Pollution: Freshwater

We all know about polluted waters. Many rivers are still full of rusting junk or flowing with toxic waste. In the 1950s, the stomach pump was the primary hospital treatment for anyone unfortunate enough to fall into the River Mersey anywhere along its course from the Pennines to the Irish Sea. However, I think that many of us missed the significance of the less obvious effluent pollutants such as run-off from agriculture or the discharge from the Port St. Mary brewery that we studied on our university field trip. However, even in the early 1960s, a BSc degree provided some professional opportunity to work in the environment. One of my friends in the Liverpool class of 1961—T. E. L.

Langford—worked as a freshwater biologist, first for the Lincolnshire River Board and then studying hot-water pollution for the Central Electricity Generating Board. He studied the effects of hot water on the coarse fishery on the River Trent in central England. His work and a book by his mentor, Professor H. B. N. Hynes, led me to realize that one person's pollution could be another's benefit. The coarse fishery in the industrial heartland of Britain is a multi-million dollar recreational industry. Dozens of people, even hundreds, line the banks of rivers and canals each weekend fishing for perch and other coarse fish. Much of the activity is competitive. The fish are caught, held briefly for verification, and returned. In the 1950s and 1960s, some of the prime sites for coarse fishing were along stretches at, and downstream from, the electricity generating plants where the warm water from cooling towers was returned to the waterways. What others called hot-water pollution seemed to be beneficial to the growth of the fish, resulting in the desired bigger catches and of course bigger prizes for the fishing competition. The plant life flourished too, although I do not know of much research on species diversity, biomass production, or the specifics of plant ecology in those streams.

Pollution—Slag Heaps

I grew up in times when the slag heaps—huge hills of mine waste rock—dominated the landscape of coal-field communities. Depending on your status and work in the community, the heap stood as a monument to the benefits or the hazards of coal mining. My grandmother often spoke of the colliery disaster at Gresford in the northeast Wales coal field that entombed more than two hundred miners. The enormous slag heap was visible from twenty miles away and seemed to stand as a gigantic tombstone to the men who died in that huge explosion. We all noticed that hardly any plants grew on the man-made hills, but hardly any people questioned the need or the wisdom of removing them. Then came Aberfan.

The world learned about Aberfan, a small village in the South Wales coal fields, on 22 October 1964 when the massive water-saturated slag heap at the colliery engulfed the Pantglas Junior School, killing 116 school children and five of their teachers. The Aberfan disaster galvanized a nation. In the space of a few years, the world came to realize that the environmental devastation around coalfields, mines, and other "resource-extraction" industries was unacceptable as a hazard to both human and environmental safety. The mountains of mine waste from the coal mines of South Wales, West Virginia, and the Ruhr, the diamond mines of South Africa, and the nickel mines near Sudbury, have all been to some extent rehabilitated using plants. Much of the progress in environmental reclamation and remediation science was only possible because of clear-sighted research to find specific solutions in the genetic resources of plants that already grew in the vicinity. The plants that did grow on the slag heaps were tested for heavy-metal tolerance and others were specifically created by artificial mutation and testing for the same tolerances. The tasks of selecting tolerant plants, production in massive numbers, and planting on the slag heaps fell to a small band of ecologists who also undertook the research necessary to ensure that the reclamation would have a high chance of success. The sites were cleared and the rubble used for road building or, on some occasions, returned underground. The new heavy-metal-tolerant strains were planted and, slowly, floral diversity is returning to what were once barren wastelands. One perhaps surprising result of this research was that when acid rain, the next problem to emerge as a threat to our environment, showed up, the research community was ready to look for aluminum-tolerant strains, even though it did not have any of the answers immediately at hand. Scientists knew that, even if they could not find a natural mutant from which to breed the needed pollution resistance, they should be able to induce changes in the inherited material (DNA), and create the required tolerance to allow plants to survive and possibly flourish in an otherwise poisonous environment. Once that was done, the new form could be produced using scaled-up standard methods of horticulture.

What we didn't know in 1953, the year in which I began formal study of biology, was that a young American biologist, James Watson, and three English physicists—Francis Crick, Rosalind Franklin, and Maurice Wilkins—had discovered the structure of DNA. This momentous event led in many directions, not least of which was to provide the power to make precise and defined changes in living systems that would lead to the transfer of genetic material from one completely unrelated species to another, and most recently to mammalian cloning. The world of genetically modified plants has arrived. The opportunities are enormous. Some say we need never face a food production crisis again. However, the risks and consequences have received little attention and history warns us to address these concerns now.

New Species and Introducing Old Species to New Homes

During our undergraduate studies, we learned other 'stuff' about humanity and plants. Centuries of international trade, particularly with the use of gravel as ballast for ships, led to the spread of many plant species from their native communities. Some were transplanted specifically; for example the uplands of Britain that had been denuded of their deciduous forests over the centuries were reforested using various conifers. Our student ecology excursions into upland areas were increasingly restricted by fences around the conifer plantations. Here the diversity was reduced more slowly and less obviously, because it took some years for the growing trees to close the canopy and reduce the amount of light reaching the forest floor. These plantations have become full-scale forests. Ironically, a new wave of environmentalism is fighting to stop some of them being harvested for the purposes for which they were planted because they have become habitat for squirrels and other furry critters. The rare amphibians and reptiles that I knew in the pre-plantation days of the Freshfield and Ainsdale sand dunes along the Lancashire coast between Liverpool and Southport are now threatened, indeed endangered, because the plantation pines have so altered the habitat that previously rare squirrels have become established as the major species. The cry is up to save the introduced pines and the opportunistic squirrels that have displaced the original stable ecosystem with its less attractive but endangered fauna.

But the accidents of alien introduction have occasionally given us a new and exciting insight into the processes of species formation. My taxonomic botany professor told of the emergence of a new species, as a result of hybridization between a native British dune grass and an alien that was assumed to have arrived in ballast from eastern North America sometime in the late nineteenth century. Research showed that the hybrid was sterile but was such a good clonal propagator that it became well established. The research also revealed that a mutation eventually occurred in the hybrid and the offspring were fertile. The result of these accidents of human activity and natural genetic change is a vigorous dune grass (*Spartina x townsendii*). The new species is now a major management tool wherever sand dune stabilization is required to protect human property along temperate coasts.

The Path to Professing Botany

During my career as a student, the research future for graduates in the more esoteric fields almost certainly required postgraduate work and, in most cases, study for the PhD was an all but obligatory path. My own research on plant proteins was technically interesting and certainly gave me an excellent foundation to grow as a scientist. The new reality was that I had followed the academic path of least resistance to nurture my lifelong interest in plant natural history but was now required to make a living.

The Botany Department at the University of Liverpool housed the secretariat of the Flora Europaea project. Attendance at morning coffee and afternoon tea was mandatory and those of us who were not in the Flora project were often asked to explain our work to visiting plant taxonomists, not to mention the department head (Professor Alan Burges), the fungus freaks, and the seaweed group. Graduate students were expected to be at all the seminars by visiting speakers, many of whom were contributors to Flora Europaea. The excitement of the impending publication of the Flora's first volume pervaded the whole department. It was a very low-key wedge, to mix the metaphors, but it maintained my interest in systematic botany. It was also a major influence on my decision to seek employment as a schoolteacher in a boarding school with a long and distinguished tradition of natural historians on its biology teaching staff, and ultimately to return to university.

The autumn term of 1964 at Blundell's School in Devon was the occasion of my entry into professional natural history. My first class was to teach remedial physics at the same level from which I thought I had been permanently released ten years before. The botany curriculum, for which I was responsible, was heavily biased to plant anatomy but I added all the latest stuff that I could from plant physiology. The required sections in plant ecology and taxonomy gave me my first chance to share my excitement about plants with young men between the ages of thirteen and eighteen who frankly couldn't care less about plants. The hidden benefit was that boarding schools have many other activities. I volunteered to revitalize the school natural history society and discovered the benefits of having students on campus seven days per week. According to their housemasters, they should be kept busy and interested so that they would stay out of trouble.

It did not take me long to discover that the archives of the school contained natural history records dating to its foundation in 1604. In addition, my students were most willing to do fieldwork. Such occasions were obvious opportunities for a clandestine cigarette or assignation with a young lady who lived nearby. The two of us on the biology staff were well known for becoming too engrossed in the wonders of the plant, animal, and microbial world to worry much about school rules. As long as everyone did the assigned team tasks and avoided risk to life and limb, the focus was on comparing our collections with the species lists from the classes of long ago, measuring the effects of water pollution, or the arrival of a new weed. We tried to find a biochemical basis for distinguishing two moss species. We measured the spread of *Lupinus arboreus* from its first introduction on Dawlish Warren at the mouth of the River Exe. We followed the eutrophication (natural infilling) of a section of the Tiverton Canal (now restored as a recreational waterway, complete with coarse fishery). We continued collecting the butterfly, *Maniola jurtina*, from two sides of a small stream at the bottom of the sports field, which was an invisible and almost uncrossable boundary between two genetically distinct populations discovered by a former teacher, W. H. Dowdeswell.

In 1967 I was offered an opportunity to start postdoctoral research at the University of Texas at Austin with Professors Ralph

Alston and Billie Turner, two of the founders of chemical plant systematics. Unfortunately, Ralph Alston died three days before my arrival and, although I learned a great deal about systematic botany, the original research program never really got off the ground. Instead, I taught in the first-year biology course and began my thirty-year love affair with plant cell walls.

From Plant Physiology via Biophysics and Botanical Gardens to Ethics

I joined the Botany Department at the University of British Columbia in 1968 and found myself among colleagues who were actively researching the life histories and ecosystems of the British Columbia flora, and had an enormous commitment to teaching. My immediate tasks were to develop my own research program studying plant cell walls, to lecture in the first-year biology course and to restructure its laboratory program. Even then the budgets were limited and the challenge was how to give 1,500-plus eighteen-to-twenty-year-olds a hands-on opportunity to study real organisms in the real world. During my time at the University of Texas, I had watched with admiration as Dr. Dan Willard organized 3,500 first-year students into a spring project program that took many of them into the field. The opportunity to destroy the University Endowment Lands surrounding the UBC campus with a similar program was real and obviously unacceptable. However, thanks to the willingness of several ecology graduate students of the day, the 1,500 students in the UBC first-year course were divided into manageable groups of between twenty and fifty students, and the "Elective Laboratory" was born. Although not all chose the outdoor experience available during March in the Vancouver area, well over eight hundred of those students did go to the field and did have at least a tiny experience of natural history research. Thirty years later, the electives are still a key part of first-year biology at UBC, and some students still recall that month in their first year as one of the more memorable periods of their undergraduate studies. An additional reward for me is that outdoor projects have become key experiences in all the first-year biology lab work at UBC. Other universities and colleges are joining the bandwagon. Such activities are often the first opportunities for students to do some real science since they were in elementary or junior high school.

My research in plant cell wall structure was very closely linked to plant hormone research. In the early years, we studied fungi, including species that were human pathogens, but by 1973 the prospects of a life spent studying detailed biochemical variation in cell wall polysaccharides had become singularly unattractive. Yet another unexpected encounter, this time with Professor R. D. Preston, took me back into physics and a twenty-year collaboration with Professors Myer Bloom and Alex Mackay, two nuclear magnetic resonance researchers at UBC. We studied the molecular architecture of cell walls and some of our research contributions have proved valuable to understanding the very complicated systems that contain most of the biomass produced by plants.

A key influence in my career at UBC was the restructuring of the

UBC Botanical Garden, which began under the direction of Dr. Roy Taylor soon after I arrived. The garden, which is the oldest continuously operating botanical garden in Canada, was established in 1915 by "Botany John" Davidson. Davidson, who had no university education in botany, was the first professor appointed to teach at what was then the new university. Roy Taylor added to Davidson's legacy by concentrating the garden's activities on the showpiece Nitobe Memorial Japanese Garden and a fifty-plus-acre site at the southwest corner of the campus. The result is the fine garden that exists today, of which I am privileged to be the research coordinator.

It was soon after my appointment to the editorial board of the *Canadian Journal of Botany* in 1980 that I encountered my first case of plagiarism and was thrust into the world of research ethics. My first editorial task was exciting and a welcome opportunity to return to the literature of real plants and natural history once again. Unfortunately, the plagiarism case came soon afterwards and reminded me of the dangers when competition to be first leads to dishonest practice. Research involves finding out things. Research requires originality and creativity. The intellectual reward is credit for the discovery. Professional science also requires dollars, and confidential proposals for funding must be subject to expert evaluation. The process is similar to that used prior to publication of research papers, but problems arise because access to a research proposal, which obviously does not have the results, becomes an opportunity for the unscrupulous to steal ideas. While the evaluation of research proposals includes ethical issues surrounding confidentiality, it also includes the often implicit question, should we be doing this kind of science? The recent, almost incredible, advances in genetic engineering and biotechnology and the public realization that science can alter the genetic composition of organisms forces science and society to consider the consequences of our newfound discoveries and skills.

The Ethical Dilemma of Genetic Engineering for Plants

In the mid 1980s, our cell wall research seemed to be leading us into the molecular architecture of wood. We tried unsuccessfully to develop laboratory tissue culture methods to clone conifers, but as we set the project aside, the world of plant biotechnology and genetic engineering burst open. Scientists learned how to move genes from one species to another, and I found myself considering the science that we ought not to do from both an editorial and research perspective.

One rose grower's dream in the 1950s was to find or breed a blue rose. We had a green rose at home (*Rosa chinensis* var. *viridis*), so the idea of a blue rose was not strange to me. The goal of breeding such a plant has been supplanted by the new biotechnological reality that genes for the production of a blue pigment can be moved into roses. That blue rose is now a reality and commercial production is imminent. In 1997 the world was surprised, one may even say stunned, by the announcement that Dolly was a cloned sheep. In 1998, Dr. Richard Seed, a physicist, announced his intention of making human clones available commercially. Human genes have been transferred into domesticated animals, and gene replacement therapy is clearly possible. Xenotransplantation—the transfer of organs between species—is a reality. The question "should science be doing this kind of research?" is now real and cannot be avoided. The defence that science can and must be allowed to proceed unrestrained for the good of humanity is no longer acceptable to society at large.

So, where do plants fit in? Surely, gene transfer and other genetic engineering of plants are not dangerous? We seem to need every advance in food production that science can provide as the world's population continues to grow at an uncontrolled rate. The use of rapeseed (canola) oil as a food oil has been made possible largely by the use of selection and genetic engineering to remove the noxious-tasting erucic acid. The development of the Flav'r Sav'r tomato is another example of genetic engineering applied to speed up the plant breeder's work. One interpretation of such research is that it is simply accelerating processes that could only be achieved by the plant breeder after many years of selection and the risk that the selection process would not succeed.

The issue becomes more complex when we consider genetic engineering that probably could not be achieved by the plant breeder. The transfers of genes between species (as in the blueing of the rose, movement of anti-freeze genes from fish to vegetables), or the creation of new genes (such as the herbicide-resistance genes) raise ethical questions that both society and scientists require us to address. The warning signs are out. The first herbicide-resistant genes have "leaked" from an engineered European rapeseed variety into the surrounding native forms. It seems that the engineers forgot about the pollinating insects.

It is indisputable that much of humanity's success on this planet can be attributed to advances in our understanding of nature that have come from scientific research. However, never before have we been able to manipulate our biological world as quickly as we currently can using the techniques of genetic manipulation, nor are science or society ready to deal with the consequences of our learning. For all the great successes of science, scientists and society have been generally unsuccessful in predicting the impact of new discoveries. In many cases, we have taken risks without even considering that the actions are risky.

There is another important ethical issue today. Many of the current biotechnological advances bring opportunities for financial gain to the industries that apply them and to the scientific researchers who made the first discoveries. Because government funding of university research is dropping and there are major efforts to replace it with money from industry, university scientists face two obligations: to produce research results that will meet granting agency expectations, and to ensure that their discoveries are adequately protected to allow the industrial partners time to undertake the development necessary to bring a product to market and profitability. The dilemma is not that industrial protection is wrong, but that science, which has worked for so many decades to convince society that it is a reliable source of objective knowledge and expertise, now finds itself increasingly dependent on funding that is an investment for profit. The public perception of such funding is that it compromises credibility, and scientists must deal with this issue.

The central dilemma, though, is science seeking ways to alter organisms in ways that seem otherwise unavailable to Nature. It is not just a question of animal rights or plant rights. The question is Nature's rights. Are we allowed to mess around with Nature just because we know how to? Can plant scientists move genes around simply because they have the tools to add to the technology of modern farming? Are we not obliged to consider our contract with Nature whether one is a retired citizen who wishes to play farmer or a scientist who could learn and apply the methods of modern molecular biology to move genes around the living world?

We can no longer hide behind the myth that all our science is for the good of humanity.

My Spirituality

Michael Aleksiuk

LET ME TELL YOU ABOUT MY PLACE, MY FOREST. IT'S FAIRLY typical as boreal forests go, and some people even say, "What's the big deal? It's just bush."

It's not "just bush." It's where I connect with the god of nature.

My cathedral is a mixed-wood forest about six miles south of Athabasca—a tract consisting of trembling aspen, black poplar, white spruce, and paper birch. Beneath the canopy lies a profusion of shooting stars, Jacob's ladder, pink wintergreen, honeysuckle vines, blue columbine, and a host of other species. Though not abundant, yellow lady slippers bloom in spots. Saw-whet owls sound like woodcutters sharpening saws throughout the night. Great horned owls hoot in the eerie moonlight. Ruffed grouse drum from almost every suitable log. Red-eyed vireos sing cheerfully on calm summer mornings. The white-tail deer is present in great numbers, and an occasional wolf trots through the area.

I discovered the forest in 1979, and immediately recognized its potential. When a quarter-section (160 acres, roughly equivalent to twenty-five medium-sized city blocks) near its centre came up for sale a couple of years later, I didn't hesitate for a moment. My newly purchased piece of Eden would be an ideal "lot" for the home I was planning to build.

There was a fully serviced road (Landing Trail) less than half a mile to the east, but my quarter-section had a wilderness flavour. I could walk anywhere on it and see no sign of the built world, a fine place for someone who wished to escape the city! After I had my computer set up and connected to the 'Net, I knew I could become a virtual hunter-gatherer there.

My property lay on the west slope of Tawatinaw Valley, facing the rising sun. There was a lovely meadow near the southeast corner, next to a couple of springs that flowed year round. One of the springs consisted of a barely perceptible seep, but the other formed a definite brook at the bottom of a ravine. An old logging road meandered from Landing Trail to the meadow, providing me with vehicular access. Though boggy in spots, it was better than no access at all. In May of 1982 I upgraded the road to make it traversable in all kinds of weather, and in late October I hurriedly threw up a tiny cabin next to the meadow, adding the finishing touches to my little hut just as snow began to fly.

In the years that followed, I became an integral part of the web of life in the forest. Ravens flew across the sky as I picked blueberries among the aspens. Sandhill cranes issued their weird croaking calls as they passed overhead. White-throated sparrows serenaded me to sleep at day's end. Coyotes howled in the distance practically every night.

Pileated woodpeckers hammered on tree trunks as I drifted toward consciousness in the early-morning stillness. For me, all these things help define perfection.

In the depth of winter the poplar woods take on a hue that somehow reminds me of death. Is this bleakness perfection? Is this greyness beautiful? So unlike the warm embrace of summer, I think as I survey the silent forest from the doorstep in my longjohns one frigid winter morning. There is a glow in the eastern sky, and the moon shines weakly to the southwest. The evenness of the snow is broken where a moose had stood as it browsed on a nearby dogwood during the night. But the cold drives me back inside, where I heap wood on the coals.

Nature's Altar

The ravine, through which the bigger of the two springs flows, is the most intimate part of my forest. Here lies my altar. The roots of a large spruce had been loosened by rushing flood waters, causing the tree to fall across the spring, providing me with a pew. Just upstream of the spruce a small waterfall has created a pool, where I get my drinking water.

It is a sweltering afternoon in August. Pleased with the progress I am making in my landscaping efforts, I decide to take a break. I make my way down to the spring, grabbing onto saplings in order to avoid sliding down the side of the ravine. The cold water from the pool soothes my parched throat as I drink deeply. I am sweaty from clearing brush, but the sweat feels good. I like sweat. Not the sweat of rushing to catch the bus, or the sweat of fear. More like the sweat of making love. For me, that can be the perspiration generated while toiling in the underbrush, making room for small spruce trees I want to plant next May. I welcome the smell of sweat when it's mixed with the fragrance of crushed spruce needles and the aroma of forest soil. It makes me feel robust and alive.

I seat myself on the fallen spruce and face west toward a willow bush that grows beyond the pool.

Was it something in the water, or is this magic real? The sun's rays are reflecting off every blade of grass, glinting off every leaf: *the forest is shining*. The slight perturbation of my arrival gradually fades, like ripples from a pebble tossed into a pond, and the rhythm of the forest returns. The stream trickling into the pool is creating water music. A wren chatters softly in a clump of hazel bushes nearby, hidden from view by foliage. A red-shafted flicker calls from a poplar above the ravine, breaking the hush in an unintrusive way. An aspen leaf moves back and forth in the motionless air. A chipmunk scurries out of the underbrush; tail twitching, it eyes me suspiciously. Seeing I mean no harm, it disappears into the undergrowth, where it can be heard rummaging among dry leaves on the ground. Reappearing momentarily with a tiny mushroom in its mouth, the chipmunk is gone as quickly as it had appeared. Two whiskeyjacks materialize out of nowhere and glide from branch to branch, looking for a hand-out from me. A mink makes its way along the spring, chocolate-brown fur glistening whenever it catches a ray of sunlight. The mink pauses and peers at me intently, eyes like beads of black ice and nostrils quivering. Then it vanishes, leaving me to wonder whether it had ever been there in the first place.

The bouquet is delicious. The spicy aroma of pine needles drifts down from above. An earthy aura of leaf litter, mushrooms, and wild mint emanates from below. The fragrance of highbush cranberries is everywhere.

Consciousness does not get much better than this. Every muscle in my body relaxes. Every neuron in my brain slows down. I feel no emotion, I experience no thought, I feel compelled to take no action. My mind is crystal clear, my senses razor sharp. I sense photons striking chlorophyll molecules in the birch leaf above my head, microscopic nematodes streaming through the humus beneath my feet. I sense electrons spinning in my atoms, Earth turning on its axis, distant galaxies reeling slowly.

Only in wild nature can I experience this wonderful state of being, and even then only when the stress and worry of modern life leave me. But the sadness passes and I luxuriate again in the timelessness of this fleeting moment.

It was there, beside the spring, that early one evening I was inspired to begin a weekly newspaper column on matters about nature and people. Reliable sources had reported that the world's largest single-line kraft pulp mill was being planned for Athabasca, and I knew there were few worse things that could happen to the area and its inhabitants (human and nonhuman alike). I had seen what the world's largest oil sands plant had done to Fort McMurray and the natural environment surrounding it, and was appalled at the prospect of something similar happening in the Athabasca area.

The development of the oil sands did financial wonders for families who emigrated from Newfoundland and elsewhere, but it shattered the lives of local folks whose ancestors had resided in the Fort McMurray area for thousands of years. Native spirituality suffered a severe blow. White residents fared little better. True, one or two became very rich, but in the process the original community was obliterated. Some people died in the chaos that ensued (including a wonderful woman by the name of Doreen Fleming). Almost everyone suffered cultural deterioration. Alcoholism became rampant. Members of the original population gobbled tranquilizers and anti-depressants like jelly beans, and eventually most of them were swept away by a tidal wave of jobseekers and fortune-hunters from the south. What had been a small town of people gently going about their lives became a drug-drenched, beer-soaked city of would-be millionaires. Whereas only recently many families in the area lived, contentedly enough, on an annual income of less than $7,000, the newcomers earned $70,000 and wanted more. Some of the original residents also took high-paying jobs. Dogsleds that cost nothing were cast aside for Skidoos that carried a $6,000 price tag. Free log cabins were replaced by engineered homes that cost $245,000.

In addition to destroying the original human community in the area, the oil sands plants desecrated the natural environment. A pristine area of rivers, lakes, and forests fell prey to over-powered motorboats, screaming dirtbikes, ten-thousand-dollar all-terrain vehicles, thundering helicopters, and nonstop traffic hell-bent for Edmonton. The water was fouled, the air polluted, the forest slashed. The fish in the river tasted like diesel fuel. When the people ate those fish, that is. Government brochures warned local residents that eating river-caught fish more than once a week was dangerous to health. Pregnant women shouldn't eat those fish at all. Much better to buy ocean-perch fillets at Safeway, the public health nurse from Edmonton said.

I reflected upon these matters as I sat there by my spring that evening. Do I want a pulp mill in the Athabasca area? Do I want to see what I witnessed in Fort McMurray repeated in this community? Obviously not, so I decided I would do my best to prevent that from happening by writing a weekly newspaper column.

Poacher's Landing

My concern about the proposed pulp mill was very personal. I was born in a log cabin near the Athabasca River, surrounded by stretches of old-growth forest. My father foresaw Hitler's hideous plan, and wisely left Europe with his young wife in April of 1939. The Great Depression was in full swing, so when he arrived in Canada my dad decided to take a homestead rather than join the destitute throngs in the city. He selected a fruitful piece of land in the wilderness, where he and my mother thrived on nature's bounty.

When my mother's labour pains began unexpectedly on 6 December 1942, it was four o'clock in the morning. A blizzard raged outside the cabin and the temperature was well below minus thirty. My father wasn't so foolish as to take a chance with the horse-drawn sleigh through the piercing cold and swirling snow, and as a result I was born at home. During a blizzard deep in the wilderness! This fact never ceases to delight me.

Nine miles northwest of where I was born there is a natural cut in the steep banks of the Athabasca River, making it possible for local residents to drive their vehicles down to the water's edge. During the Dirty Thirties, and even as recently as the 1950s, many people in the area relied heavily on wild game and blueberries as food sources. Moose were commonly hunted by boat on the river—in and out of season. In order to avoid detection by Frank Farrell (the game warden), folks discreetly loaded their poached meat onto wagons and pick-up trucks at this secluded spot. The location eventually became known as Poacher's Landing.

As it turned out, the proposed pulp mill was to be situated at Poacher's Landing.

Partly because I was born nearby and partly because it was a beautiful setting, I have gone to Poacher's Landing often since I returned to Alberta in 1976. Not as a poacher, but a nature lover. No one landed moose there any more. Instead families went to the site for occasional picnics by the river's edge on Sunday afternoon. Young lovers went there late at night to watch the moon reflect off the water. I frequented the location because it was important to my serenity.

I got up from the spruce log and headed up the side of the ravine. I had an urge to begin my column immediately, without delay. But first I wanted to visit Poacher's Landing. Who knows, I reasoned to myself, it might be my last visit there (that in fact proved to be the case). I drove toward the Landing, some twenty miles away.

The Athabasca is not a big river, like the Mississippi, or a great river, like the Yukon. But it's my river, and that makes it special to me. You can put a canoe into the Athabasca at any point downstream of Jasper National Park, and paddle all the way to the Arctic Ocean. Back in the 1950s, I often sat on the bank of the river and day-dreamed of paddling deep into the northern forests. In 1959, at the age of sixteen, I had what was for me an almost unbelievable opportunity to spend my summer holidays on this river. I worked for the Alberta Forest Service, cruising timber during the long summer days. And I was paid for it, too.

Those days on the river back in 1959 were the old days, and we did things the old way. We had no radio contact with the outside world. Only rarely did we see an airplane overhead. Three or four times we saw a DC–6 on its way to Yellowknife. Once we heard a small bush-plane somewhere to the south. We encountered only one boat other than ours during the entire season: Dick Neumann, a furtrader based at Pelican Portage, passed by our tent camp with his riverboat, headed upstream toward the town of Athabasca for winter supplies. Apart from the faint drone of an occasional airplane and the ten minutes it took Neumann to pass our camp with his ancient scow, it was a wonderfully silent summer. Today it's not uncommon to see three or four vapour trails in the sky at one time, and powerful jetboats pollute both the silence and the river every weekend.

These were some of my thoughts as I drove toward Poacher's Landing that evening.

Finally I was there, sitting on a boulder and gazing at the river like one sometimes gazes at one's sleeping lover. A river is more than water flowing over mud and rocks. A wild river has a definite spirit that is easily detected by anyone who looks at it with care. I looked at my river, I looked at the forest and the wildness. The river was alive, pulsing audibly in the fading light. A warm rain was coming down ever so softly, almost like a mist, and the evening air was potent with the fragrance of wild things. As I sat there, I wondered how you say goodbye to a river.

My weekly column, entitled "Nature, Environment and People," ran in a regional chain of newspapers from 1988 to 1990. In it I tried to put the proposed pulp mill in perspective for the people of the area. Based on the extensive environmental and social damage I had witnessed at the oil sands projects near Fort McMurray between 1976 and 1986, I addressed critical issues surrounding large industrial developments. I focused on interrelationships among three entities: (1) all of living nature; (2) those portions of nature the public often terms "the environment" (air, land, and water); and (3) humans as an integral component of nature. My ultimate objective was to make it clear that humans are part of the natural order, and that what hurts nature also hurts us.

Apparently the powers-that-be couldn't, or wouldn't, see the truth through the dollar signs in their eyes. Ralph Klein, then minister of environment within the Alberta government and currently premier, grinned broadly at me one day and remarked, "You must be one of those university types!" Then he became more serious and said, almost angrily, "I don't know anything about the natural order, but I know plenty about social disorder. I know people need jobs."

The Altar of Mammon

The pulp mill project—Alberta-Pacific, abbreviated to Al-Pac—went ahead, and began operating in 1993. Poacher's Landing still exists as a physical site, but as a shrine it's dead. The same is pretty much true of the river. I'm glad I said goodbye while I had the chance. I'll never go to Poacher's Landing again, precisely because the mill stands there like a gigantic tombstone. I'll not go to that pulp mill, for in my mind it represents the antithesis of everything that is natural and good. But the pulp mill came to me, like a predator bent on capturing its prey. A predator whose teeth are made of shining steel. In 1995 my forest and the inner peace that came with it were shattered by a man who serves the pulp mill's purposes exceptionally well.

When I purchased my parcel of land, the quarters to the north, south, and west were covered by continuous forest. Like mine, the quarters to the north and west are still fully clothed, but the one to the south has been stripped naked, ravaged, and left for dead. Clear-cut, that is.

Before I relate the details of how one of Mammon's disciples violated the sanctity of my forest, let me give you a better picture of the local setting.

The original bush trail that I upgraded to provide all-weather access to my cabin branches just at the point where it reaches my meadow. One branch heads up the hill, to the west, and meanders through the ravines and ridges on my land. It is an old haul road that had been used by local loggers during the first half of the twentieth century, when people in the area logged with horses and for the primary purpose of constructing their homestead buildings. I removed the alder, birch, and hazel shoots that were beginning to invade the haul road, thereby creating a hiking trail through what is a jungle humming with life in summer and a silent wonderland in winter. The other branch of the trail continues southward along the public road allowance past my meadow. Until 1995 it was not traversable by car or truck during the summer months: it was merely a boggy remnant of an old wagon road that dates back seventy-five years or so. My meadow was thus at a dead-end insofar as an all-weather road was concerned. Perfect. No traffic went by—*ever*.

The old logging road across my quarter is safe; because it is on private property, it can't be altered by anyone. Not legally, anyway. I allow everyone to use it as a hiking or equestrian trail, but I suffer no one to desecrate it. The wagon trail proceeding south past my meadow is quite another matter. Because it is on a public road allowance, it's vulnerable to abuse. From the moment I realized just how precious was my nature retreat, my greatest fear was that someone would buy the quarter south of mine and create a gravel pit or perhaps set up a sawmill. The quarter to the north is mostly muskeg. While of major interest to one who appreciates nature, it is of no value to a developer or to a person looking for a building site. But the south quarter is all high ground. The forest there was thick and mature, and underlain by known gravel deposits. What if someone bought the quarter and developed it? For years I was nervous about the situation.

Then, in 1995, it happened.

One morning in late January I drove up from Edmonton to spend a few days at my retreat. As I turned off Landing Trail onto my access road, I noticed huge vehicle tracks in the snow. Some sort of truck had gone in, and hadn't yet come out. I eased the car into my meadow, and saw that the truck had proceeded on to the south quarter. I turned off the ignition and got out of the car. Rather than being met with the deep winter silence to which I was accustomed, the grinding rumble of a bulldozer and the crash of falling trees assailed my ears. Chances are you haven't heard the sound of large trees being felled by a bulldozer. First there is a powerful roar as the bulldozer's engine revs up in the process of pushing a tree over. Then the noise level subsides slightly as the bulldozer slacks off and the tree falls through the air. Finally, the tree hits the earth with a tremendous thud that makes the ground shake. The whole thing is reminiscent of the sound of a tornado moving through a forest, interrupted at intervals as the bulldozer backs up in preparation for its assault on yet another tree.

My heart sank.

I got back into my car. There would be no serenity here today. Maybe there never would again.

But perhaps someone had bought the quarter and was just preparing a building site. Perhaps it was even a nature lover, like me, for that was an exceptionally idyllic quarter. Maybe he's (or even better, she's, for I'm single) a kindred spirit, I thought hopefully. I decided to go see Tony, who at least until recently owned that quarter, to find out what was happening. I knew he also owned a bulldozer, and it was conceivable he was clearing a building site for the new owner (if that was indeed the explanation). When I pulled into Tony's yard fifteen minutes later, his pick-up truck was parked in front of the house and the bulldozer was visible in its usual place near the machine shop.

I knocked on the door to his house.

"Come in!"

When I walked into the kitchen, Tony was seated at the table—looking sheepish but unapologetic.

The long and the short of it was that the quarter had been purchased by a logger from Plamondon, a community fifty miles to the east. A logger by the name of Steve. The man was planning to clear the entire quarter, sell the trees to the pulp mill, and then create a gravel pit. He hoped Al-Pac would buy the gravel as well as the trees.

Dejected, I drove slowly back to my place.

This news was too depressing. I didn't even get out of my car, but instead followed the loop through the meadow and headed back to Edmonton. There was no point in sticking around. If I stayed and watched, I'd feel like a parishioner standing by helplessly as vandals demolished part of the church. I couldn't do that, so I drove home.

After the initial shock, I was simply numb. Maybe things would eventually settle down and I'd get used to the devastation on the south quarter. The gravel in the vicinity was rumoured to be of poor quality. Too much sand and clay mixed in with it, some said. Maybe the gravel pit wouldn't materialize, and, except for the cleared south quarter, conditions would eventually return to near normal. Things would never be the same, but my soul would heal. The scar would always be there, and it would always be sensitive, but the throbbing pain would be gone.

A couple of weeks later I went back to see how much damage had been done. I approached from the east side of the Tawatinaw Valley, where I would have a good view of both my quarter and the one being clear-cut. As I came to the edge of the valley and proceeded down the slope, I saw that the entire south quarter had already been cleared. There was a gigantic row of logs lying across the width of the quarter at the upper end, and a second row lower down. Much as my mind didn't want to accept what my brain perceived, the truth was there, plain as day.

Not Much Good for Anything

When I got to my place, a bulldozer was ripping up the earth on the public road allowance between the meadow and the south quarter. They were apparently creating a haul road for the trucks that would move the logs to the mill. As I got out of my car and approached the bulldozer, the operator turned the engine off. Dense smoke ceased to pour from the exhaust pipe. The silence that ensued was wonderful.

The man got off his machine and walked toward me. He was about thirty-five, with a long and somewhat scraggly beard. Sandy-blond hair. In spite of the fact that the air temperature was below the freezing point, he was wearing only a hooded sweatshirt over a regular shirt, and the hood was down. The man was boyish and gentle in appearance, but I could see he was in an aggressive mood.

"Hi, I'm Steve," he said without offering his hand. "You own this place?"

"Yes."

"Good. I've been looking for you. How much you want for it?"

"It's not for sale."

He seemed surprised.

"You sure? I'll give you a good price."

"I said it's not for sale."

"Well, okay. But tell you what, how about if I buy just the trees. That way you'll make some bucks and still get to keep the quarter. By the look of that shack of yours, you could use the money. I've got the equipment here and everything. Might as well go for it, man. I'll buy the trees where they stand. I'll clear the entire quarter, and sell the trees to Al-Pac. Like I said, you'll make some money and get to keep the land too. Not only that—the quarter will be worth something after it's cleared. It's not much good for anything right now."

I felt like telling him to get out of my face; instead I said I wasn't interested. I went on to say they'd better start hauling the logs out, as the spring thaw was just around the corner. The road would be getting soft soon. He said yeah, he knew; they were going to start hauling next week. He got back onto his bulldozer, fired it up with a deafening roar, and continued ripping the road surface. I puttered around my place, but, with the dozer working one hundred yards away, it was no good. I got into my car and drove to Edmonton.

When I came back in late March, the logs had not been moved. They were still piled in two rows, clearly visible from the east side of the valley. On inquiring at the Rollings' (my neighbours), I learned that Steve wasn't satisfied with the price he'd been offered at the Al-Pac mill, and was looking elsewhere. This of course meant the logs wouldn't be moved until the next winter, for during the summer my road would not stand up to the weight of logging trucks. Good, I thought. Maybe the logs would rot and Steve wouldn't be able to sell them at all.

Spring arrived, the grey forest turned green, and my pain began to subside. Spring turned to summer. When I sat there on the fallen spruce before the little pool, I managed to experience some peace.

Then one morning in late August, just as I approached my access road after a relaxing drive from Edmonton, I saw a loaded logging truck turn onto Landing Trail. They were moving the logs! I stared in disbelief as a stranger with a scraggly beard and sandy-blond hair wheeled the rig in a wide arc and headed toward Athabasca.

What about my road?!

I drove toward my place, and immediately saw getting in with my car was out of the question. My road had been ripped up by the bulldozer in order to form a clay base for the trucks. Mounds of dirt were heaped everywhere. Even with the clay base, the weight of the trucks had created deep ruts and rough ridges. Destruction of the forest had been hard to take, but it was legal. My dismay was not something with which county officials would sympathize. They would in fact ridicule the notion of spirituality having anything to do with "bush." Their god was in the church in town. Actually, the Al-Pac mill had become their real god.

However, destruction of public roads was something to which county officials could relate. I backed my car out onto Landing Trail, turned around, and headed straight for the county office in Athabasca. After hearing my complaint, the public works manager reluctantly phoned Steve (the manager obviously sided with the logger, but because of legalities was forced to take action on my behalf). Steve's permit to haul logs over the public road was rescinded until December, when the ground would be frozen. Furthermore, the manager informed Steve he would have to upgrade the road's condition to the point where I could traverse it with my car, and requested that he meet me there within three hours.

Steve was loathe to spend money on the road for my benefit. But during our initial meeting to discuss my access needs, he assured me the road would be in perfect shape within a few days. A part in the bulldozer was broken, he added as an afterthought, and needed to be replaced. He would purchase the part in Edmonton on Monday (our discussion took place on a Friday), and the road would be in tip-top condition by the end of next week—for sure.

When I went there seven days later, nothing had been done. At first I was livid, but after fuming for a while I decided it might be wise to take a diplomatic approach. Instead of going back to Edmonton, I drove out to Steve's place near the village of Plamondon. During our discussion the previous week he had invited me to "drop by sometime," so I decided to drop by. I've always been fond of Plamondon, a sleepy community located at the west end of Lac La Biche (a beautiful body of water). I have pleasant memories of the beach there in 1960, late at night. Doris Gauthier, a lissome girl whose father had had a mink ranch on the lake shore during the 1950s and 1960s, still occupies a special place in my heart. Though almost entirely a French community prior to 1965 or so, Plamondon was later settled by a large group of White Russian families. Steve was a member of one of those families.

God's Children

The White Russians in the former Soviet Union had resisted the changes wrought by the Russian Revolution. They wanted no part of Marx or Lenin or the secular way of life espoused by the Bolsheviks: they liked the way things were, and refused to change. They believed deeply in their culture. They clung to the old Orthodox religion, and continued to follow the Julian calendar. When the pressure to change became increasingly difficult to resist, large numbers of White Russians left the former Soviet Union and moved to Brazil, Oregon, and Canada. They went not as individuals or individual family units, but as entire communities. During the 1960s and 1970s, dozens of White Russian families settled on farms in the Plamondon area. In addition to farming for a living, they undertook various logging projects. As is typical of White Russians throughout the world, they kept to themselves. They chose not to integrate into the pre-existing French community at Plamondon, and retained essentially all their cultural heritage.

Those White Russians remain true to their culture to this very day. They speak Russian, even though they haven't lived in Russia for decades. The Christian god reigns supreme; the Orthodox faith of medieval times shows no sign of loosening its grip. Christmas is celebrated on January 7th, New Year's on January 14th. Those folk are as closely knit a group as they have ever been. On warm summer Sundays they gather at Beaver Lake for communal picnics. The children play on the beach, the men discuss commerce, and the women prepare food and gossip.

However, in one area of their lives the White Russians of Plamondon are modern: they embrace advances in technology. They especially love big tractors, big bulldozers, and big logging trucks. Machines are something they understand. The nonmaterial aspects of their culture date back to the sixteenth century and before, but the White Russians are quite modern when it comes to farming methods and tree-harvesting techniques. And it doesn't stop at farming and logging. Recent electronic innovations, such as cellular phones and fax machines, are welcome too—especially among younger people. Indeed anything that will help them make money, that has prestige value, and that will give them status is avidly pursued.

When it comes to material culture, Steve is more modern than most. As I turned off the highway toward his spacious yard, I was amazed to see that the driveway was paved right up to the house. A paved driveway on a farm! That has to be the only one in the entire region (the others are made of gravel). The man himself stood beside some roof trusses he was fitting together. He later informed me he was building an addition to the house in order to create a new master bedroom. And that bedroom, Steve bragged, would have an open-beam ceiling. I drove up the slight incline from the highway to the house, parked my car to one side of the trusses, and got out. Steve was obviously pleased to see me.

It was a warm day in early autumn, with a hint of yellow in some of the trees. Steve squinted into the sun and sort of smirked. He knew his place was quite a contrast to mine, and was proud of that fact. We exchanged pleasantries, and within a few minutes Steve offered to show me around. The yard was filled with the trappings of "success." A new half-ton truck that must have cost $45,000 was parked front and centre. A newish Cadillac was parked nearby. There was a sleek motorboat mounted on one trailer, and two "jet skis" (also known as "personal watercraft") straddled another—ready for action on Beaver Lake. A "quad" (four-wheeled, all-terrain recreational vehicle) and a Skidoo were positioned further back. What looked like a garage proved to be a beauty centre Steve's wife Eva had set up for the women in the community. What appeared to be an expensive garden shed with cedar siding was really a sauna. The land on which Steve's fancy house stood was anything but humble: to the southeast, Lac La Biche stretched placidly into the distance.

I steered our conversation in the direction of Athabasca. I pointed out that what he had done to my road was like someone coming in and ripping up his paved driveway with a bulldozer. When was he going to repair the damage he had done, I asked. Oh, he didn't have the part for the dozer yet, he replied. Why didn't he go and pick it up today, I countered as I looked at the truss he had been piecing together for the extravagant addition to his already large house. Well, he had phoned Edmonton this morning; the part wasn't available yet. He would phone again on Monday . . .

It wasn't until the end of October that my road was finally touched up enough to give me the all-weather access I needed.

I got to know Steve quite well in the weeks between late August and late October, and found, in spite of everything, that I almost came to like him as a person, and if you met him you'd probably like him too. As well, in a way, he is part of nature, as a logger, as a man more instinctive than I am, a kind of natural man. He goes with the flow, while I am fighting the world. But in another way he is destroying the world that gives him his living, and destroying the environment we all need. To him, my spiritual home is just bush to exploit.

This whole incident illustrates to what a degree personal values can have an impact on the environment. If we are to make sustainable progress as a society in a way that preserves the biosphere, societal values will have to change.

Footnote: A Downstream Effect

All the above material was written in January of 1997. I added the words in this final section on 25 June 1998.

Like Poacher's Landing, the quiet pool where until recently I sat and experienced a deep sense of connection with nature still exists. However, again like Poacher's Landing, the pool is no longer a source of spirituality for me.

The flow that created the pool is a true spring. The water is wonderfully cold, and, in addition to being nice to drink on hot days, it keeps my food and beverages chilled even at the height of summer heat. In April of 1998 I placed four quarts of canned crab apples at the bottom of the pool.

When I took them out to eat I was puzzled by the heavy silt that had buried the jars at the bottom of the pool, but didn't give the matter any serious thought. The organic debris was puzzling too, but I simply swept it out of the pool with a spade and thought no more of it.

When I returned a week later, the amount of sandy silt in the spring had increased dramatically and the pool surface was covered by organic debris. The little brook at the bottom of the ravine was running high from recent rains. Closer examination revealed the debris to be made of crushed material from trembling aspens (mostly bits of bark and decaying wood).

The week after that, portions of the tiny channel were completely silted in. Where until recently there had been intricate mosses, mysterious little horsetail-like plants, elaborate liverworts, freshwater sponges, fancy fungal growths, and other wondrous things along the channel, now there was only silt. Where sparkling water had flowed through deep recesses below moss-covered logs and among polished stones, now there was only silt.

It was obvious what had happened. Over the past twenty years, this little brook had contained nothing but crystal-clear water. Unfortunately, the ravine in which the brook lies crosses the quarter-section to the south before it comes unto my property. Steve's quarter-section. In the process of clear-cutting his land, Steve had torn up the earth along the ravine and crushed countless rotten aspens under the steel tracks of his tree harvester. During periods of rain, rushing waters wash silt and crushed wood down from his quarter-section onto mine, a classical downstream effect. My ravine, with its once-sparkling spring and little pool, may fill in to the point where I won't be able to use the water for domestic purposes any more. And sadly, I no longer find the spring and its immediate environs a source of spirituality.

Earlier, I thought Steve had only damaged my peripheries, but now I know he got me in the heart. I am of course deeply saddened by the effects of Steve's actions—firstly because of the unexpected impact of his materialism on my spirituality, and secondly because of what this seemingly minor incident represents at a global level. The cumulative effects of millions of such "minor incidents" represent the deterioration of the biosphere.

Body Shock

Aritha van Herk

I WAS ONCE STRUCK BY LIGHTNING. WELL, ALMOST STRUCK BY lightning. I was twelve years old, living on the central Alberta farm where I grew up. It was five in the afternoon, I had gone to the pasture to get the cows, to bring them home for evening milking. This was a task I enjoyed, for I could escape the bent-back tension of weeding the garden, I could drop my hoe and rake, I could abandon the mower in the middle of the lawn. Getting the cows meant a ramble to the back of the pasture, gopher holes to investigate, tall grass brushing my knees. It meant looping the edge of the slough, happy ducks diving into green algae. And it meant walking the cows home the long way, around the back of the quarter, through the parkland poplar stand tangled with wild roses and saskatoon bushes and poison ivy. The cowpath through the brush was worn to a dirt thread, and the cows followed it with that benign dignity cows practice so well. I was free to follow them through the sun and shade of field and trees, running or jumping fallen branches, stopping at a whim, listening to tree-rustle, and indulging in my day-dreams.

The heat of summer afternoons often brought on thunderstorms, a conference of dark clouds riding low in the sky, pushing through the thick air to explode into rain or hail, sometimes rolling past with only a growl of their cumulonimbus weight. To say that I loved and still love thunderstorms passionately is to speak the obvious. There is something about the heavy pressure of sky, its dense buffet of air against air before the release of rain, and then the quickened cooling of drops smattering against the ground, soaking straight through clothing, that invigorates like nothing else. I confess that I dream of living in Buitenzorg, Java, where it thunders, they say, some 322 of the 365 days in a year, more than any other place on earth.

I knew all the advice about thunderstorms. Stay inside. Or shelter in a thick copse of trees, under the shortest ones. Crouch close to the ground. Avoid high places, isolated trees or telephone poles, wire fences and water. I paid attention but I didn't care. Perhaps I wanted to attract lightning, wanted to feel that terrible surge of heat through my bones, wanted to have a shouting match with the baritone voice of Thor.

I was bringing the cows home. The sky had been rumbling for an hour, undecided about whether to rain or not, full of gloom and prophesy. There were a few distant strikes, the thunder following *sotto voce* as if it were counties away. The cows already through the fence and on their way into the barn, I was lingering, waiting for the rain.

Suddenly is not sudden enough for the suddenness that confronted me then, introducing to my stunned body a noise as deafening as a giant whip, a crack, a boom, a dreadful sonic thud. Before my eyes, perhaps three yards away, and as if on the heels of its announcement, lightning, a divine finger of revelation, forked the ground in front of me. I felt my hair rise, my clothes tearing themselves from my body. I felt the ground shake, felt in a thousandth of a second currents of light, a green flash, an electric shudder. A long still breath and then the sky flung out a sheet of rain.

Weak to my knees, I could utter no sound. I wanted to bolt into a run, I wanted to laugh and cry, I wanted to catch hold of that single stroke and ride its coriolis effect, I wanted to dance in the rain. I could only sit on the ground touching the wet grass, my hands against the predictable earth. A few steps farther and I might have been dead. But I was untouched, merely shaken, as if the body shock I had been given was a nudge rather than a strike.

I didn't tell my parents. Why distress them when I was alive? But the bolt that might have erased my consciousness, the almost-blow I did absorb, that intense and powerful collision, imprinted itself to the very marrow of my bones. I hold its dark shimmer as close to memory as I can, and try to revisit that sudden burst of light, that revelation.

What does such a concussion bestow? Reflectiveness, creativity, a gift of sight? I suppose I have always wanted to believe that the lightning singled me out to shake me awake, to remind me of its power, to brand my memory. It was a warning. Don't try to erase nature's electrical charge from your skin or your breath. Don't forget that wind and rain and lightning will always overpower even the imagination. It was a blessing, a gift, a sharp, booming stroke of enunciation about the power of enunciation.

Such moments of recognition, human connection to natural epiphanies, are far too glibly lost. We are inclined to predicting and manipulating and fussing about the weather. Our support of weather-vanes and weathermen, our avid reliance on satellite photos and radar, carries a weather-sickness that is—if we bother to stand back and observe—ridiculous. Why not look out of the window instead of turning on the television to "watch" the weather?

But if our desire to predict the weather is understandable, our desire to control it is more sinister, clearly a mark of some hubristic contemporary sense that all matters are controllable, or at least available to be controlled, whether they be money markets or ageing, traffic patterns or that vast and mysterious ocean of air that we swim against. We take for granted the oxygen and chlorophyll that sustain us, we are unwilling to countenance flood or drought or the variegations of rain, the seasonal visits of insects, the hesitations of saskatoon berries. Such arrogance, as Rachel Carson has said, is born of a strange conjunction of biology and convenience.

In a world where the effects of weather are routinely erased from our lives, the body begins to believe that thunderstorms take place in words, that cloudshine plays beyond the window, and that sunrise and sunset are choreographed for a schedule rather than for the real turning of this real planet earth. We are too easily house-bound, too readily do we tailor our schedules to weather. Unlike the character in Charlotte Bronte's *Shirley*, who "took walks in all weathers—long walks in solitary directions," we hesitate to step outside without umbrella or sunscreen. Estranged from the immediacies of nature, frightened of their having an effect on our serene disregard, our paranoid self-protectiveness, we do not walk at all.

And yet, nature has a way of stepping inside this invented insularity, of reminding humans that there are still movements of earth and sky large enough to make us blink and pay attention. Hurricane or flood, drought or ice-storm, fog or flurry, will subvert predictability, insist on the waywardness of surprise. And why should the air be benign, merely invisible? In an ounce of air, scientists tell us, there are more than 1,000,000,000,000,000,000,000,000 molecules, including nitrogren, hydrogen, oxygen, carbon dioxide, bouncing against one another, energy and excitement in every jostle and touch, every figurative conjunction. Is this a lifeless world that we can ignore, pretend inanimate? Only to our peril. The sky embraces its own activity, complete with dust and viruses, gravity and seedlings. It is as alive as any mammal.

And the sky is home to the wind, the same wind that seeped into my pores as a child, that spoke a story when it touched my face. I loved to run to the pasture, or to the very back of my father's land, because I could wrestle with the wind, its sudden gusts, its exhilerating push. I lived with the wind as if it were a favourite coat or game, a playmate. Running into the wind, I experienced an exhileration that I have never been able to duplicate, not in driving, or in flying, or even in writing. Caught in an embrace of air, feeling that rush, wind hands parting or tugging my hair, I came to know a pleasure unmeasurable, erotic, as powerful a caress as that of any expert lover. When the wind blew, I would sneak out to the bush pasture, and in an act of pure defiance, take off my shirt and shorts, stash them under a stone, and run, as close to naked as possible, with the wind.

The wind is really many winds, and these winds have names, but to me, it was The Wind, an invisible flame that I leant against, pushed into, surrounded myself with. Whoever wrote the line "the wind our enemy" has no agreement from me. The Wind was a soothing friend, lifting from my shoulders the burdens of childhood and growing up, suggesting incipient transformation. This wind is as present in Calgary now as it was in the parkland of Alberta then, but I have less dialogue with it. It has become something I register between car and building, or out for walk, something that I speak to less freely, confined now by the principles of age, and an urban lack of privacy.

But this wind still taunts me, dares me to revive my younger self and to run again toward its Aeolian charm. I live in a house perched on the brow of the wind. Well, it is a height of land, but the wind seems more present than the ground, it groans and sweeps, it calls and buffets, I hear it riding high off the edge of the foreland thrust sheets that are the foothills of the Rockies. I listen for its sudden voice, I take in the bend of trees, a swirl of leaves or ripple of grass, and know that my friend the wind continues in its restless, cryptic journey, waiting for me to follow.

And when a gale-force strikes, complete with hail or snow, the character bites of smoke and water, I know the wind is seeking to remind me that I must put on a windbreaker and get outside, walk into its funnel of fury and feel again that passionate arousal. A good storm is as creative a gesture as a story or a song, a good storm is a tonic to a lazy body and a passive mind. Storms have convinced me of many things, helped me make decisions, swept clear a muddled train of thought.

The wind, our conscience, our cousinage. Camped on an esker, a clear-swept ridge, in the Mackenzie Mountains in the Yukon, I learned the pedagogical power of wind. There were five of us, with three tents, well equipped and ready to settle in for a field season. I was cooking for a geological crew, and happy to be away from the distractions of "city," with a box of books to read, and enough of a stove to cook relatively well.

The second evening, the wind began to demonstrate the Beaufort scale against which it is measured. It shifted from calm to a light breeze, stepped up a notch to a moderate breeze, then a strong breeze. It was travelling its own katabatic trajectory, in an increasing crescendo, determined and incremental, relentless. By dark, it had become a near gale, by midnight a strong gale, and by four in the morning a violent storm. We did not call it a hurricane because we could not diagnose the force—only withstand its measureless power. The wind was measuring us. I braced myself and tried to hold the shuddering tent pole to prevent the tent from blowing down, the canvas collapsing around me. A half hour at most, I thought, and the wind would die, extinguish itself. But it refused, blew with a ferocity that battered every idea of wind I had ever imagined. This was a wind to compete with my lightning bolt. It raged and tore and shoved, howled and keened. Finally, as if it had merely been warming up, this wind lifted the tent and me within it and flung me through the air, bringing me and the tent down some ten feet away in a heap of canvas and clanging metal poles and sleeping bag and scattered socks and books. The wind picked up that A-shape of man-made shelter, and the human within, and simply dropped the entire concept enough of a distance away to make a definite statement.

I lay there, stunned, under the shrieking air, feeling for broken bones. Only bruises. There was nothing to do but huddle against the ground, curl as small as any hillock of earth, as toughly rooted as a tuft of grass. In the morning, we straggled out to survey a scattered camp. All the tents were down. The metal equipment box had been turned end over end; axes and serving spoons were buried inches deep in the ground. The wind had picked us up and flung us down the hillside as casually as if we were a handful of sand. Lesson one. And yet, I wanted to stay there forever, and I and marked the spot as the place where my ashes will be spread.

But such pronouncements do not require travel to the remote Yukon mountains. The earth can bump, drop just enough to jolt the stomach even when we are safe in bed, the covers warm over our shoulders, the pillow a soft slice of dream, drifting in that other world, the one we live in when we are asleep. I was certainly asleep—asleep in my bed in a room in an apartment in a larger apartment block in the middle of a western city, asleep in that hour just as dawn is about to commence—a deep intense sleep where dreaming is vivid with detail and where the body wages its own secret discoveries and astonishments.

The window rattled. The curtains swung. The bed beneath me rumbled, stirred, then seemed to absorb a distant beating, a percussion section hammering deeper than deep in the bowels of earth. I struggled to wake myself enough to recognize this subterranean echo, its powerful throat-call, and distantly, distantly, felt the bed, the floor, the building, the very clay holding the building's foundations, shudder. An earthquake in northwest Calgary, completely irrational in terms of fault zone or expected tremor, utterly idiosyncratic. And yet, entirely possible.

It woke me up. I woke and knew I had felt the hollow undulation of the earth's crust, a seismic rupture. The giants buried by Jupiter were restless; the tortoise carrying the globe on its back had heaved a sigh. The oracular earth was asserting its salt. I lay anticipating another convulsion, the solid plate of the gyromantic ground demanding that the body of humanity pay attention, *habeas corpus*.

But the moment was over, the profound perturbation I had felt now quiet, the feverish ground still again. How to return to sleep after that awakening? How to recompose the sleeping dream after that quake, its volutation? The substratum of solidity had lurched, and we who had registered its stagger in that pre-dawn light were foundlings, reminded again of orphanhood, of dispossession. Lying there, in bed still, the floor and furniture exactly where it always was, I felt my bones shift in a faint registry of awe. Such a fracture refuses to accommodate invisible, pliable, erasable nature. This was a reminder.

Writers, of course, are supposed, even required to practice a hyper-awareness that ignores nothing and observes all, antennae tuned to subtle registries, quick to smell the presence of ghosts. We need to be trapped in a thunderstorm, we need to experience an earthquake in order, finally, to overcome words, to transcend their crafted dismissals, to meet the doubtful self within the zone of articulation.

I knew this body shock most certainly the night that I slept on ice. Already language fails. It was not night, since it was late May in the Arctic, and at that time of year day is virtually extended to twenty-four hours of daylight, winter almost benign, a reliable twenty below, mild compared to the intense temperatures of the winter dark when the windchill will reach sixty or eighty below. So it was not night, although I slept. And I slept, although I did not sleep at all; my sleep was on a bed of ice, that ice an eerie drift riding the ocean currents between Devon and Ellesmere Island. Both are in the High Arctic, beyond the near and the far north, part of the polar ice-cap, a moving grinding pan of congealed salt water that refuses to melt despite the temptations of lingering summer light.

We were travelling from Resolute Bay to Grise Fiord, some six hundred kilometres, travelling across land and frozen water on an Inuit *komatik*. We were destined for Ellesmere, the most northerly island in the Arctic archipelago, Ellesmere notched by fiords and aproned by sea ice, a true polar desert, miraculous in its living sparseness. And on the way, we camped on the ice of Jones Sound, that long and narrow elbow of ocean connecting Baffin Bay and Bear Bay and Norwegian Bay, a sounding separating Ellesmere from Devon Island.

There is certainly a tide under that ice, and I could hear it following the moon as I lay there in the strangest cradle of all. I was encased in down-filled long underwear, and huddled within a down-filled sleeping bag that rested on the superlative insulation of a fine caribou skin spread on a four-inch-thick artificial foamy placed squarely on a canvas tent floor. The tent was pitched on some four inches of snow that had hard-drifted across the ice, ice frozen solid six feet thick, as oddly and murkily clear as if it were a green mirror. Below the ice swam five hundred feet of polar water, water so cold it could melt skin and break bones.

I slept in that cryptic bed and knew myself silenced. And yet, I was visited by a eulalic and ecstatic articulation, the noses of char and seal bumping against my dreams, the swish of fins and the secret crystallization of snow making me, in my physical recognition of my own tongue-tied and limited speech, at last expressive, at last able to write my body shock.

My body shock was not brought on by cold or fear or even time.

It was the idea of sleeping on ice, the fact of sleeping on water without the hull of a boat to keep that water away. Magic was surely born out of such a paradox. Yes, there were layers of fur and skin and cloth and insulation between me and the ice, but the ice and I were asleep together, dreaming together, breathing and moving together. I had travelled days to find that ice, I had planned for months to meet its frosty exhalation. And finally, in that sleep, we found each other in each other's embrace, a woman trying to live and think and write in Canada meeting her destination. Ice will not tolerate tergiversation. I remembered that I was just a warm-blooded mammal, asleep in the cold/warm arms of nature's grace.

I hardly slept for the terrible joy of my night with ice.

And if you do not revisit ice often enough, it will come to you. Ice inevitably seeks me out to remind me that it is time to meet nature again, to converse in the language of nature itself. Hailstorms will do that, arrive as suddenly as spring, as unsparingly as wind, messengers of ice. When hail begins, it is sporadic, as if joking, a few shards pelting the green growth of summer in a wintry tease. They are small, hard prefigurations at first, like miniature bullets, scattering and melting as if pretending to be hard rain. But as the convective cloud lowers, the hail solidifies, pebbles itself with the glaze of its own freezing, bouncing up and down within a cloud, pushed by an updraught, pulled by pressure zones. Stones began to drum with a passionate clatter, the noise of a spilled bag of marbles across a floor, increasing in crescendo to roar, crash, rattle, impetuous stones denting whatever will take their shape, tearing through the thin cloth of July leaves and flowers. This hail is aggressive, intense, a shout, a drum, a battlefield. I might look for a wedge of blue through the clouds, the quick shift of the sky's eye, but my garden will be shredded despite my supplicating watch, my promises to renew my neglected covenant with ice.

I've collected a few hailstones, held them down on my bread board and carefully sawed them open. They are layered, like onions or bulbs, alternating shells of opaque rime and clear ice, as if a metaphor for words, the ice a distillation of supercooled rain droplets, the rime opaque, dense beingness that remains mysterious, uncapturable, unlanguaged. Precipitation. All forms of precipitation start with water vapour, begin under the auspices of condensation, of which only 20 per cent reaches the earth. To condense then, is to build from magic vapour—the diaphanous, the ethereal—a real result, moisture. As the writer, struggling with all that is vainly imaginative or whimsical, which is fleeting and insubstantial, seeks to make an idea. As the writer must find a way to say: lightning is as quick and electric as lightning; wind is as brisk as wind; rain is as wet as rain; earthquakes grumble like earthquakes; hail is as sharp and cutting as hail; ice is as cold and precise as ice.

And nature behaves like nature, complex beyond description. This continent of human thought is carnivorous, dolce, dolorous, ubiquitous, risible, adamant, capricious, funny, seductive, erratic, dependable, elemental. It bends from the waist to offer a surprise, to give complacent me, one bare forked animal, a quick, sharp shock, a body shock reaffirming my membership in the natural world. Just when I think I have stepped inside the door into reliable shelter, the screendoor banging behind me having given me indemnity, I am reminded of ice and its long embrace. Nature's body shock is my *memento mori*, that beautiful conclusion teaching me to embrace nature's eloquence. Again.

The Arctic Habitat and the Integrated Self

Robert G. Williamson

Before the Onrush: A Young Man's Arctic

THE DAMAGING GLOBAL CLIMATE AND THREATENING ECONOMIC dynamics which are increasingly affecting the world are so extensive, complex, and awesome in total impact that it seems almost preposterous to inject into the picture a personal perspective, but the purpose of this book is to express individual insights and feelings. Thus it is with some sense of both temerity and justifiable modesty that I presume to set out as I have been invited, to write about the Arctic as I first found it as a young man over forty years ago, and about how it has changed up to the present. It was a time of travelling by dog-team and boat in those earlier years, and sharing the tent and iglu-dwelling life of the Inuit, visiting, hunting, and trapping, and the continuous intimacy with the habitat which was the lifeway of virtually all of the indigenous population.

It was the people who drew me there. I wanted to know the Arctic people, as they saw themselves. And by persistence and some luck, I was there, incredibly, barely twenty, on my own initiative, with all my youthful adventures of the mind now close to reality. My presence there was not an ego-based projection of some consciously defined self. I was too young, too wide-open to impressions to be self-aware, avidly experiencing sounds, scenes: the saline sniff of the summer sea, the tidal creak of winter ice, the smell of freshly hunted meat, the keen whip of the wind, and best of all, the fascination of the people's language, the shared joy in their children, and the frequent laughter. Kindly laughter, from the gut, honest, hearty, spontaneous, satisfying as a good post-prandial belch. I lingered among the Inuit, my English schoolboy self diffused and lost happily amidst these welcoming, competent, confident folk. It was what I dreamed of.

Like most British boys, I had grown up on a rich reading-diet of 'English' hero adventuring around the world, but what caught my interest most was the polar travel. However, I became gradually aware that some of these heroes were most distinguished by their mindless courage, or to put it another way, their courageous mindlessness (and sometimes, plain arrogant stupidity). They were adventurers, and brave certainly, but also opportunists, preferment seekers, colonizers and frequently intellectually and socially inhibited or unenhanced by racial double standards. Some were like the wooden-headed, blindly Britannic Sir John Franklin who went to his death and left two ships' crews to die with him or after him, rather than divest himself of the habits of his English self, and learn from the local people. So I started to read about them, the Inuit. Then I needed to read about how to really understand their cultures; and so began, at the age of twelve, my life-long adventure with anthropology. Before I had been thirteen very long, I had laid aside the journals of Scott and Shackleton and Cherry- Garrard and Belcher and the Ross brothers and Parry, and was being carried along by some of the anthropological greats, Malinowski, Von Gennep, Fraser, Evans-Pritchard, Mead, Benedict, Firth, the Kluckhohns, and Boas, the "father of North American Anthroplogy" and, most significantly for me, also the author of *The Central Eskimo*. I was later to learn that some of these, like Radcliffe-Brown certainly, and even Boas, lived through their times and made their contributions still tugged in their personal behaviour by an undertow of double standards. But the intellectual absorption was deep. Anthropology was already more than a discipline. It was the daily means of understanding people as culturally conditioned. It was a way of life.

So when Lord Mountevans offered me a chance to go to the Antarctic on an expedition of which he was patron, I was able to say politely that though I was already committed to polar travel, it was not to study ice or geology, meteorology or aurora, but to live with and learn from people. And soon thereafter I came to Canada, heading north. That was very early in January 1952. After a short stay with friends in Ottawa, I was lucky (or brash) enough to convince the president of the Northern Transportation Company (1947) that I would be an excellent acquisition as boat-crew working down the MacKenzie, northward to the Arctic Sea. I travelled the whole length of that Great River as purser several times. Always I was looking for chances to learn from the local people (whom it was part of my job to meet), and find a way of staying with them when freeze-up came. And I did it. I found employment at Fort Simpson, NWT in the northernmost experimental station in Canada (closed down long ago). I spent the winter reading anthropology, and taking a few dog-team trips, while documenting Dene folklore and folk-tales, the substance of my first professional publication a couple of years later.

That winter I volunteered to go to Baffin Island to help build a house commissioned by the Anglican bishop—not because of any profound claims to personal spirituality (and Bishop Marsh was certainly not a spiritual inspirer), but because he thought I could hold a hammer by the right end and read a blueprint the proper way up. Later of course I discovered that the local Inuit were better at both than me—but the bishop's double-standard judgement paid my way there, as I was willing to over-winter in the Arctic for many months before house-building could begin, something most regular working carpenters would be unable to contemplate. For me it was a unique chance.

Those were the days, it should be remembered, when contact with the northern posts was by means of ship, once a year. One single ship accomplished the delivery of supplies for the fur-trade post settlements, the repatriation of patients who had been south in sanitoriums and the evacuation of those needing treatment, and the replacement of northern agency staff (policemen, fur traders, missionaries returning from or going on furlough)—all during one short visit at what was known as "ship-time." By the time the ship arrived and everything was squared away for the winter, it was too late to start house-building, the winter starting early in the Arctic, and I had many months of time in which I could invest a lot of energy in the learning of the language and travelling by dog-team out with the hunters and to the hunting camps, learning the way of the life of the Inuit.

Language Acquisition

I was most fortunate in being able to learn quite early in my life among the Inuit the indigenous mode of habitat relationship and self-perception, essentially because of my keen interest and lucky facility with language learning. Previous reading about perceptive cognition, worldview, and language had reinforced my logical aversion to the few Inuktitut language-learning aids then available (lacking, as they did, the desirable indigenous logic). Almost all were missionary products, and every published source I consulted, including also some non-missionary efforts, approached the description of the language in the mental framework of the classically trained grammarian, thus pre-structuring their material with Greco-Latin grammatical categorizations and linear thought. I chose to rely on a felicitously sensitive ear, an open-minded capacity for contextual grasp of vocabulary, and word-choice (socially, emotionally, and situationally), and lively enjoyment of the language-acquisition process and interpersonal communication momentum. Simply overhearing the language while verbally uninvolved was perhaps the most instructive learning experience, because native-speakers talking to each other naturally make no effort to simplify or restructure their speech, as often they may do for newcomers. So, the depth and variable realities of the language are more readily available to the keen conversational listener.

Of course four decades ago (or a century ago, since the whaling era) travel into the Arctic, even by the one annual supply ship, was already a long-established form of southern industrial intrusion into the region. It was part of the southern assumption of the appropriateness of human-being imposition (claimed as the work of superior creation, indeed God's likeness and spiritual vessel) upon the environment. But on my first seven-week voyage through the Eastern Arctic on board ship in the late summer of 1953, were Inuit passengers, mainly people on their way home from southern sanitoriums, but there were also some others being moved from one Arctic location to another. The cultural context in which they lived conversationally transcended the temporary southern-made "big ship" setting in which they were for that travelling time. And with the initial help of a quick-minded and scientifically unschooled Newfoundlander (and ex-fur-trader) who had a huge and easy "natural" facility with the language (the widely beloved Leo Manning), and a missionary rare in his Anglican ranks as a skilled but nonpedantic Inuktitut speaker with good accent and tonal quality (Rev. Donald Whitebread), I began to enter the Inuktitut world. (Both these helpers are long ago deceased, sadly, and I owe them a word of thanks.) I was twenty years old at the time.

The language "Inuktitut" provides a number of valuable language insights, such as the genderlessness of the essence of a person, and the fact that the same word (Inuktitut) is applied not only to language but also to the identification of beliefs and values, technologies, and material culture styles. So it was that, as I moved geographically into the Arctic, I was being prepared perceptually for the relationship with the habitat of the people who lived unmanipulatively as an integral part of it. Soon after, arriving in Pangnirtung, I began to see the real Arctic—not from the height of a ship's deck where I was unable to "hear" the environment because of the machinery and alien voices, but from the midst of natural habitat. Already I was beginning to realize from my listening that the Inuit lived in a multi-dimensional cognitive setting that integrated places and people through their system of place-naming. (Later I was to learn of the enormous significance of the associated soul-name system.) As time and travel and comprehension extended, I was able to develop some factual depth beyond my early impressions of Inuit perception of the habitat.

The Spirit of the Habitat

I had seen physiographically the low-lying land-reaches and driftwood-strewn beaches in the region around the MacKenzie Delta, and the rolling tundra and rocky outcrop country of the Hudson's Bay and Hudson's Strait lands, and the majestic alpine heights and soaring fjords of Baffin Island, Ellesmere, and Devon, and gravel-patch islands and occasional cliff-side eminencies of the High Arctic—all with the eye of the boyhood reader of "explorer" travel. I entered the Arctic with the joy of one vividly experiencing the vibrant air and flourishing animal, bird, and plant-life of the mid-summer season as the ice was breaking. But very soon I began to realize that for the indigenous people their habitat is so much more than landscape, ice-scape, and sea-scape. Essentially and crucially, the habitat of the Inuit is name-scape. Geographical features of course have generic descriptor terms, but almost every island, headland, bay, hill, lake, river, glacier, escarpment, cliff-foot flatland, and polynya also has its own specific name or names. Some places have several names, variable according to angle of approach, tide, season, local form of activity (fish-jigging, look-out, food-cache, caribou ford, hunting side, seal basking place) or specific individual historic event. Most important is that many of these places have personage or family associations, some of very long standing, far back in the generations of the group. So the names, I realized, are group-held metaphors from whole historic experiences. The inspired and insightful British scholar, Mark Nuttall, talks about "memory-scape" (*Arctic Homeland: Kinship, Community and Development in*

Northwest Greenland, University of Toronto Press, 1992), a most appropriate term, and his are the best analytical contributions to the circumpolar literature in a generation.

Naming

More recently I have concluded that for my purposes the term "namescape" is also very useful, because memories are often triggered or indicated by names. Certainly naming in the case of the Inuit is particularly significant, both for physical features and in the context of metaphysical beliefs in which names are vitally involved individually and integratively. In fact every geographical feature, and especially its name, is a living, continuously significant symbolization of the collective experience of the local group. And insofar as the individual realizes herself or himself to be, and is perceived by other group members to be, related to that name and what it stands for in local historical understanding, each individual is secured and reinforced in personal identity. At the same time, people are integrated into a network of memory and kin-type commitments. I say "kin-type" because people who are not kinsfolk are often functionally and emotionally drawn institutionally into relationships of kinship-like significance. This occurs among the Inuit through the bonding of the *sauniq* system, or by meat-sharing partnership, or by other forms of what is often inappropriately called "fictive" kinship, but which I would term functional kinship. *Sauniq* means bone, literally, but it also means name-partner, sharer of the same name. This implies a great deal, in that *sauniit* (plural) are part of the specific life-force and character of a revered and beloved soul, actualized by the name.

"Fictive kinship" is, of course, a mode of bond-creation in many cultures, including the European and Euro-North American ones, possibly increasingly so in the mobile and atomized and fractured world of modern society, where nucleated couples feel impelled to create their

own family atmosphere by conferring kinship terms on close friends. Usually these are people with whom they have more in common than with their own relatives. But in Inuit society this bonding terminology has always and anciently been seriously committal, not only in terms of mutual and material and emotional support, occasional gift-giving and even life-sustaining responsibility, but also in terms of the metaphysical relationship through the soul-name system. This in turn links the individual to the many-named habitats, so that among the Inuit no one ever feels alone in the Arctic. It is not a "barren waste" nor an unoccupied hinterland, but the habitat of a complex network of souls, all active socially and spiritually in the life of the people.

Listening carefully and understanding better gradually, over time I learned the nonlinear, nonsequential way of thinking that allowed for admission into narrative, folk-tale, or personal reminiscence at any point, without the constraints of the time-logic patterning of my own culture's language. Concurrently I discovered the lucid, multi-dimensional pure logic of Inuktitut, a cognitive pattern which makes the person thinking in that language feel secure both in abstraction and in concrete expression. This is made possible by the holophrastic or compound-coordinative-word nature of the Inuktitut language. Insofar as the language is the intellectual and emotional mode for enabling relationship with the physical habitat and the social environment, and integrating these dimensions, I began to understand the attitudes the Inuit use to live effectively with their setting. It is a set of feelings which are both quietly confident, based on deep knowledge learned daily from infancy, and quietly accepting vicissitude and hardship, again drawing on intimate environmental knowledge, and the sense of belonging to, rather than being alien to, the setting.

I learned, through analysis of the language and increasingly better-informed inquiry, about the cosmological context in which the Inuit perceived themselves, and the way this related to the named habitat and the way the beliefs are integrated with the system of values. The first and perhaps most important concept I learned, because of its pervasiveness in daily speech, belief and action, is the notion of *Sila*. Superficially I quickly realized that it was the word for weather, and the outside. But in time I was taught that *Sila* most essentially means the great creative force, the life-giving power, the vital animating spirit which envelops all creation and in which we all dwell and which dwells in all of us, and thus is shared by all living creatures and organisms. It is the air, without which there is no life; and it is no less the essence of intellect. An intelligent person is said to be *silatujuq*—well-endowed with the animating spirit, and as a value statement thus the highest of compliments. (Equally, *silaituq*, the negative form, is strong criticism.) At the same time I was learning that having the capacity for thought—

isuma—is an essential quality sought for in responsible people, and so I came to understand why the word for leader is not "strong man" or "skilled person" but *isumata*—thoughtful person, one who takes thought. Thus, simultaneously I was learning the cosmology, something about the traditional beliefs, and also the interrelated system of values.

It was the naming system that gave all of this cogency, amplitude, and connectedness. I remember this important aspect of Inuktitut belief and behaviour being brought home to me vividly one Arctic night when visiting an old man, for the moment alone in his iglu. As we talked, his granddaughter came in, pushing ahead of her the five-year-old little girl who was her daughter. The old man addressed her as *attaatatsiak*, which I knew means grandfather. Shortly afterwards, when receiving genealogical data, I noticed that the child's name was the same as the old man's grandfather's name. Soon the pattern became discernible that virtually all people were named after predeceased individuals, usually within the extended family network. It was also apparent that children tended to be named after someone very recently dead.

The fact that Inuktitut names have no gender is salient. Children were named after someone who had recently died, regardless of gender. By now I had learned that in addition to belonging within the life-giving context of *Sila* (which condition we share with all living matter), every person has *tarniq*—individual soul. I had learned that cosmologically, creation began out of darkness and chaos and the random swirling of cosmic powers, when a chance concatenation of powers caused the emission of a word; and when that word happened, all creation and its relationships and cadences fell into logical place. Thus a word is more than an abstract symbol; it is a full reality in its own right, and once articulated goes on existing as all realities do. A name is of course a word, and thus everyone's *tarniq*, soul, is in fact a word. Soul and word-as-name-are inextricable realities. Over my years in the Arctic the rootedness and cognency of this belief was reiterated for me in many forms, contexts, and happenings. It is when one realizes the social and metaphysical importance of the soul-name system that one also realizes the significance of its relatedness to the habitat name-scape. It becomes clear that exterior-society tinkering with this naming system was disintegrative and damaging on a cosmic scale of cultural significance.

Explorers

The first to impose alien names, displace traditional names, and generally evince no great regard for names that called forth one of the most deeply felt Inuit values—personal respect—were the so-called explorers. These new arrivals from Europe, venturing into the Arctic first of all in search of trade routes to the Orient (the "Northwest Passage"), tended to commemorate themselves or their patron sponsors or monarchs and aristocracies in their map-making. Worse was their practice of designating large areas, intimately known and named by the indigenous people, as *terra incognita* or *terra nullia* ("unknown land," "empty land"). This misuse of human habitats that were neither unknown nor empty I regard as nugatory, insulting, and essentially an initial symbolic justification for alien incursion and exploitation. I have called the practice "toponymic colonization."

In the nineteenth century the explorers, now less often mercantile adventurers and more frequently members of the British Royal Navy, some of them avoiding half-pay on the Inactive List after the end of the Napoleonic Wars, further penetrated into the eastern Arctic. The western approaches were largely not investigated by the southern ships until after the egregious Sir John Franklin got lost (with two ships' crews) in 1848, and remarkable navigators like the Scots Captain McClintock came around the Horn and into the Arctic Ocean by way of Bering Strait. (Many of the better Arctic navigators were in fact Scots). Indeed, much of the "official" mapping of the Arctic in the nineteenth century was done by Royal Navy officers looking for employment, promotion, trade routes, glory, and each other.

These mercantile and Navy people were admittedly often brave and enterprising, but they were certainly not the original explorers (or discoverers) of the Arctic. The Inuit had not only explored the Arctic, probably beginning at least five thousand years ago, but they named it, very extensively, and carried from generation to generation the most detailed and accurate mental maps of the region as part of the oral tradition, cosmology, and belief system. Words like "first explorers" or "discoverers" gave the earnest but often insensitive Englishmen a cachet that helped to justify the colonization of the region. Those who for five millennia had ranged the Arctic without the help of European technology, raised their families and developed their culture in that habitat, are much more deserving of recognition. And in the process they developed philosophically a quite different sense of self than that evinced by the egocentric thrust of Franklin, and earlier people like Hudson, Davis, Frobisher, and later Norwegians and Frenchmen and a few Germans. These European men were driven by strong personal and nationalistic ambitions upheld by determined individual egos—in sharp contrast to the quiet, self-effacing, soul-autonomy-respecting Inuit who often submerged self in a collectivized identity. They lived with their habitat as sharers in *Sila*, rather than seeing themselves as leader-conquerors of a great alien space. Indeed, in a society that survived essentially through long-term co-operativeness, the competitive spirit of the self-asserter was not valued, and appropriate behaviour was nonaggressive and self-denigratory. *Isumata* stature came with recognition of knowledge acquired over many years, or exceptional intelligence employed with subtle skill, sensitivity, and respect for other bearers of respected souls. This soul respect allowed at the same time a remarkable degree of autonomy for individuals of all ages, and considerable tolerance of eccentricity and foible.

The Whaling Era and Exteriorization

Over the same nineteenth century period as the British Royal Navy excursions into the Arctic increased, a more widely scattered, dynamic, and ultimately more influential element was coming into the country—the whalers, funded from the US and Britain. Whale oil and baleen were in great demand in the nineteeth century. Commercial whaling had actually begun out of Europe much earlier, with small numbers of Basque and later Dutch crews moving, after the loss of whale populations off the Iberian coasts, to the North Atlantic and notably to the Baffin Bay waters off western Greenland. The worldwide boom in whale hunting developed early in the nineteenth century, and as more accessible populations of whales diminished, the search reached into the rich fields of the polar seas. Encountering the Inuit when watering, coasting, or returning to the home vessel in their bow-at-each-end, clinker-built, oar-propelled whale boats, the Europeans developed a symbiotic relationship with the indigenous people. First using their local knowledge of whale movements and behaviour, and soon going on to employ them as pilots, boat-men, flensers, and general labourers, the whalers became increasingly accustomed to working with the Inuit. They often returned to the same coasts year after year and employed the same people, who for their part valued the goods (knives, pans, needles, guns, ammunition, fabrics, flour, and baking powder) which they received for their services. Over time these goods became standard parts of the indigenous lifestyle, and even though they faced the virtual certainty of widespread contagious illness every time the whalers came back, most Inuit continued to welcome them. Others remained out of direct contact with the whalers, but traded for their goods through go-betweens.

The symbiosis that developed became further institutionalized by the beginning of the second half of the nineteenth century, when the whalers took to wintering in the Arctic so as to be early on the hunting grounds after break-up the following season. This was because it was increasingly difficult to fill their holds in one short season of open water, as the whalers continued to decimate their prey populations. Inuit families were hired to supply fresh meat and clothing skins, and to sew and maintain the whale-men's clothing. They went on to work as crew or whaling-station workers the following season, and ultimately formed a core group of indigenous people almost as dependent on the exteriorized economic forces represented by the whalers as the whale-men were themselves. Latterly in the whaling era, the Europeans took to some fur-trading to supplement their declining incomes, taking advantage of the fashion changes in the great urban centres, now consuming more fine furs and fewer coarse pelts. Thus they paved the way for the fur-trade era which became patterned around sedentary trading posts as the whalers faded away in the first two decades of the twentieth century.

This process of exteriorization, which is dependent upon or vulnerable to powers and events far removed from the impacted people and often minimally understood by them, also had a depersonalizing effect upon the people, while introducing cultural values which began the process of social differentiation in a previously egalitarian society. Many ex-whaler Inuit families became socio-cultural brokers and economic instruments for the fur traders. New identities began to emerge, and with them increasingly entrenched name usages. Often the whalers gave the Inuit nicknames of their own coinage (Wager Dick, John Ell, Starb'd Eye) because of their inability or unwillingness to use the Inuit names. Mostly these were temporary working-day labels which the

Inuit used in association with the whites and dropped when out of contact. But they familiarized the Inuit with the notion of secularized, non-connective naming, with gender loading and no spiritual significance. They signalled their sense of the significance of the individual self, ephemeral in the impermanent and virtually foundation-less life of the peripatetic seaman. It was a new notion—not necessarily of a socially supported autonomy, but of individuals as ultimate isolates. This set of influences furthered the secularization process earlier begun as the Inuit observed representatives of a basically European culture, worthy in Inuit minds of respect for the intelligence indicated by their complex technology—living as they did through the Arctic winter without recourse to the supernatural beliefs and practices which they had previously considered vital to survival.

Exteriorization and Secularization, Twentieth Century

The whalers and fur-traders also provided transport and sometimes even material assistance to another powerful and much more spiritually disintegrative force which became a seriously influential part of the twentieth century Arctic society—namely the Christian missions. From the outset (beginning mostly early in the twentieth century, though some were established late in the nineteenth century), the missionaries launched a direct and profoundly significant attack on the Inuit (pagan) traditional naming system. They sought to replace the old names with baptismal names taken from the Bible or from their own European societies. (No less than in many other parts of the world, the missionaries tended to equate their cultural habits of "civilization" with Christian moral wholesomeness.) Thus, paradoxically, the missionaries had a secularizing effect on one central part of Inuit spiritual life, and promoted individuation of self and the Christian soul, in the process differentiating them from their complex network of affiliations and supports normal to preconversion life.

This secularized approach resonated with the values and financial organization system of the fur-trader, who wanted to encourage individual entrepreneurial competitiveness among their trappers. The seasonal debt practices were, along with the rough approximation to names the Inuit proffered, normally individuated. This was an accounting measure, but it also served to give more isolated identity to people. Meanwhile the missionaries followed the practices of their European cultures, and used gender-linked baptismal names for a people among whom the idea of a genderized soul was alien, indeed primitive and divisive. Then, when the Royal Canadian Mounted Police came into the Arctic early in the twentieth century as Sub-Registrars of Vital Statistics, they acquired their name-lists from traders and missionaries, and, adding their own often linguistically inept renderings, proceeded to formalize and make official the disintegrated name-self which was being institutionalized among the Inuit by the exterior society. The whole Inuit administrative system was further dehumanized in the later 1940s by the introduction of Eskimo disc numbers—identity numbers coded on a regional basis for each person—so as to make the handling of administrative tasks like the family allowance and social assistance more 'efficient'. This was the normal procedure for over a generation, and only much later replaced, by the Northwest Territorial government "Operation Surname" whereby the Christian European patriarchal notion of "Head of Family" (always male) was formalized as the source of family-naming for everyone.

The Impact of Illness

All this was happening while the Inuit society was undergoing deep and extensive stress caused by widespread illness (mainly tuberculosis) and frequent fragmenting of families as the sick were taken away to distant treatment centres (mainly in the south), sometimes for years at a time. The story of the callous herding of patients into the southern sanitoriums, with kinsfolk separated and people sometimes lost (occasionally to die and be buried in unmarked graves), is one of appalling insensitivity by medical administrators and despairing disintegration experienced by the Inuit.

Illness and the fear of illness was everywhere in the Arctic in those days so often spoken of as idyllic. The era of mainly upper-respiratory sickness on an epidemic scale coincided with the decline of the fur trade. These were epidemics of measles and diphtheria and poliomylitis too, and pneumonia often developed from influenza or common cold contagions brought in from the South. Nothing in my memory of that era was so emotionally deep-reaching as the impact of illness on the people. The remoteness and inaccessibility of the Arctic had for millennia protected the Inuit from the infections that ranged the rest of the world, and so they had not developed immunities. A mild outbreak dismissed in the South as merely a children's illness made people of all ages dangerously febrile and measles presaged pneumonia, and pneumonia killed.

Tuberculosis is a lethal and insidious disease. People can carry the bacilli in their lungs for years, encapsulated in a calcified coating until the body is severely strained by poor nutrition, prolonged cold, damp, and stress. It is a disease that is easily communicated by coughing, shared drinking vessels, even conversational moisture. And everyone lived in single-room, snow-protected dwellings, sitting and sleeping on the communal bed, and quite unaware of the concept of germs and their volatility. As the trapping deteriorated in many parts of the Arctic, and in some areas there were winters of poor hunting, the combined circumstances were ideal for the spread of illness in Inuit society. Add to that the complete absence of doctors living in the Arctic except at two missionary locations, and barely more than a couple of nursing stations, and one can understand how case-finding was so slow, and treatment even slower. Early in the 1950s, the Eastern Arctic Patrol (in fact a Hudson's Bay Company supply ship and later a Department of Transport vessel carrying materials and people to and away from the settlements), was augmented by a medical party consisting of a doctor, a nurse, and a radiologist. This was the federal government's response to a long-standing need, and as the awful extent of the epidemic dawned on the Ottawa-based administrators, the measures taken were incredibly hasty and insensitive. The task was to find cases by x-raying everyone while the ship was unloading. Cases were herded into three-tiered bunk rooms or holds in the ship—and taken pre-emptorily away for treatment in southern sanitoriums. Sometimes they were not even given time for family farewells or the opportunity to make arrangements for those left behind. The scenes where a mother or father or beloved child waited quietly together for the imminent moment of parting were equally poignant. So often the TB condition was so advanced when it was found that the patients' prognosis was already poor. Many never came back. Record-keeping was shoddy, and geographically and culturally ignorant. Relatives sometimes never heard what had happened to their loved one.

This circumpolar TB pandemic reached virtually every family. It was the time of the most profound alienation of the Inuit sense of self—which had always been a sensitive relationship of land-based group identity which made people feel secure in their personal autonomy. Now they were taken away from home and habitat, thousands of kilometres to the south—and, afterwards, often for years, their feet never touched the earth. They were transported many days or even weeks of sailing away to southern institutions. Medical staff, without the ability to talk with them, often settled for the impersonal case approach, so many pills, so many times a day, surgery, slow, regularly monitored by uncommunicative recovery, often entailing months flat on their backs in wards full of strangers. They had gone from ship to ambulance, to a hospital, huge and awesome, bigger than any structure they had ever seen before, taken along bewildering corridors, up and down alarming elevators, and then left to wait. No contact with the ground, no smell of the sea and living tundra. Anyone who has been ill remembers the sense of isolation and helplessness. For the sick Inuit in southern institutions so much that made up the elements of self-certainty (family, habitat, food, familiar dialect, laughter)—all were gone. And beyond the institution's windows—no familiar loom of land and sea and sky. City dreck, huge heaving trees, smoke, traffic, and strange, unnerving sounds and smells. No wonder so many died—not simply from illness but from loss of certainty of self. And when, after years of waiting, the fortunate ones got back home on the same fear-ridden ship, some having lost a lung or a kidney, and the vigour of living, too often they found family further decimated. Life also had inevitably gone on without them. Spouses sometimes remarried, believing their partner dead, their children were ageing strangers, and their valued old folk, long-beloved and needed, passed away, their bones lying beneath their rock-piled surface graves.

It was a dreadful, alienating time, the mindless and mechanistic medical system gradually succeeding in curing or repairing the ravaged Inuit bodies, but returning them to a spiritually decimated society, leached deeply of self-essence and zest of life.

The most restorative factor was the habitat. It had been always there, waiting for the soul-drained need of the hurt Inuit to move again into its ambit, returning to the places where the old souls were also waiting to be invoked. I remember an aeroplane landing on the ice near a hunting camp, returning some people from hospital. Among them was a young hunter, his hospital pallor contrasting with the bronze spring-time glow of the faces greeting the new arrivals. He asked about the whereabouts and situation of his family. Sadly the people told him his wife had died during his two-year absence in the sanatorium, and their two children separately sent to a missionary residential school.

He spoke earnestly to the owner of a dog-team that had come out to meet the plane, a kinsman's concern and understanding written on his features. And right there and then, straight from the aircraft onto the ice, he drove the borrowed team off into the surrounding country, promising to return in a few days. He drove that team nonstop, except for pauses to rest the dogs and hunt for them—for two days and two nights, and did not sleep until the third day. As we watched him heading over the ice and up the coast until he was out of sight, we understood.

The restorative relationship with the land is no less deeply needed by the modern quasi-urbanized Inuit, all across the Arctic, on into the generations following from those hurt people. That habitat-bound process of seeking renewal is going on.

At the same time the Canadian government was cooperating with the missions in taking school-age children to exile institutions, often far from home, for southern-style schooling and regimented hostel 'care' by mission staff—some of whom have been recently (1994–97) revealed to have been serious and criminally culpable child abusers. These terrifying residential schools were also organizationally the scene of severe discipline, wherein young siblings of different sex were strictly segregated and even punished for seeking each other out. Again, traditional or pagan identity usages were firmly eliminated, and mission-imposed names insisted upon, all of which accomplished a significant diminution and truncation of the self as conceived by the Inuit.

The Growth of Government

During the same era, roughly from 1953 when the Canadian Department of Northern Affairs was set up, to the late 1960s when the Territorial government in Northern Canada assumed larger powers (centralized in Yellowknife, but still mainly funded and ultimately controlled by Ottawa), other major social changes were taking place. Encouraged by the governments, and motivated by the need for access to health services and the desire to keep their children in local schools, once they were built, in the rapidly growing settlements, the Inuit moved into the trading posts and set up ship-time scrap wood shanties along the beaches. Men (as individuals, unlike the normal cooperating hunting groups) obtained casual work as labourers in the short-lived local construction booms that followed the inception of the DEW (Distant Early Warning) Line and the substantially expanded aviation services which developed along with it. Airstrips and local roads were also built. These sporadic employment booms were occasioned by the arrival of area administrators, teachers, economic development officers, social workers, and many southern-originated technical staff. Most of these expected (and largely received) urban-style housing and services. Housing programs further reinforced the quasi-urbanized dynamics thus set in train. All of this activity increased employment opportunities, brief and impermanent though many of them were. Following camp-life patterns, substantial parts of extended families crowded into these government housing units, but the administration's intention was to nucleate the dwelling patterns, thus further atomizing the traditionally group-oriented sense of self. Even the house spacing, in identical units built in straight lines, often far from the sea edge people were used to, and designed by southern engineers, divided off family and generations heretofore mainly accustomed to the single group space of the average family iglu or tent. The housing was a powerful psychological influence on the atomization process of current Inuit society.

One Canadian federal government initiative which proved useful was the inception of cooperatives in the Arctic settlements. In the first years, producer cooperatives were started, using materials and values familiar to the Inuit (for example, fisheries and indigenous arts and crafts). They involved the sharing of effort and goods for the greater collective benefit. Later, consumer cooperatives went into retail business. These cooperatives required the acquisition of macro-social organizational techniques (for example, boards of directors, committees, chairpersons, treasurers, secretaries, voting procedures, and record-keeping), which later proved useful as the settlements assumed increasing responsibility for local government. There also developed instruments of regional governance (for example, school boards and health boards) and in the process growing practice in representational politicization. These democratizing processes also had the effect of individualizing leaders, elected by competitive ballot, where previously leading personalities were typically self-effacing, and decision-making consensual.

Most significant in this context was the growth, not so much of formal parliamentary processes (into which I was drawn), but the brilliant burgeoning of what I have called Inuit 'para-political' organizations. These, such as Inuit Tapirisat of Canada, the Québec Makivik Corporation, and the Inuviaaluit of the Beaufort Sea littoral communities, became skilled at influencing governments through broad public presentations of their aspirations, while patiently reasoning with the Ottawa power mandarins (bureaucrats and national politicians.) They learned well from the movements of the federal administration negotiators, and became adept and flexible tacticians, sometimes changing approaches surprisingly and broadly but doggedly never losing sight of their essential territorial, indigenous-constitutional, economic, and governance objectives. They were at least as effective politically as the two lone Members of Parliament for the two parts of the Northwest Territories, or the elected Members of the Territorial Legislature. These forms of representation did not exist for the Central and Eastern Arctic until the 1960s, and numerically and politically they were rather limited. Still, the formal legislator role proved to be one way in which the Central Arctic Inuit of the time saw me as an instrument capable of bridging the way from micro-social traditionalistic organization to constitutionally larger involvement in mainstream national governance.

Individual Roles and Personal Integration

Here, the discussion curves round to the personal part of this present theme. The Inuit had taught me the strong positive value for love of the habitat, and the value for intelligence and for one's responsibility to use that quality. So when the Central Arctic was first enfranchised, for Territorial Legislature purposes, the local leaders said I must make available my knowledge of both cultures for the use of people. I stipulated that all of us must learn the legislative procedures and the Inuit take over of the 99 per cent indigenous constituency as soon as possible, because I personally had no political ambitions. (I represented five thousand people dotted about in seven settlements in a constituency the size of all Saskatchewan). I had long been working in the Eastern and Central Arctic regions, problem-solving, doing what amounted to applied anthropology. I had founded and edited the first Inuktitut language journal published by and for the Inuit, and I had had a pioneer hand in Inuktitut language broadcasting. Through the Canadian government, I had maintained a wide-ranging correspondence service in Inuktitut, and travelled everywhere across the Arctic, dealing with a multitude of human concerns. Later, I planned, set up, and developed, with the Institute of Northern Studies of the University of Saskatchewan, the year-round Arctic Research and Training Centre (ARTC) in Rankin Inlet, the first of its kind anywhere in the Polar world. From this base I did my research and facilitated the work of many other scholars from across the country and around the world. I conducted a number of applied anthropology courses at ARTC, courses attended by students from many parts of the North and from other countries. I also invited other scholars from my own and other institutions in a variety of disciplines to offer courses. So, one way or another, this explains why

I was not unknown and was called to rally around with the people who had given me so much. But I kept my word, and withdrew from the Legislature role as soon as possible, having helped the preparation of a good range of potential successors.

The key operational factor for me in the Legislature of the Northwest Territories was that then (and so it is to this day) the Member is elected and serves in her and his own personal right, without party affiliation. That freedom from party stripe or control was important. So a person serving in the NWT Legislature, and also now in the Nunavut House, stands individually judged and chosen, essentially involved on the basis of personal qualities associated with one's name, not national party policy or regional grouping.

There is in the Inuit culture an entrenched habit of allowing people, from infancy onward, a great degree of personal autonomy, based on the value of soul respect. Thus a person grows up not constrained by the society's physical and metaphysical networks, but rather has a sense of belonging and support, with, however, considerable flexibility and freedom of individuality. *Isumaminik*—"it's whatever a person thinks"—is a frequent nonjudgmental phrase in the society, such that only damaging behaviour, not eccentricity, is the normal focus of sanctions. Social control is dedicated to harmony and conciliation, not retribution and punishment. Thus the power of the spoken word is seen as an instrument of correctional compromise, or behaviour modification, varying from teasing, to mild gossip, to sharp ridicule. Another technique is the obverse of speaking contact—the imposition of non-speaking, nonvisiting, nonsharing ostracism, which is dire and deeply depressing. Public lampooning bouts, poetically expressed but potentially devastating, were also resorted to. It was within this well-developed set of institutions or systems of behaviour, subtly inherent or clearly articulated in the language, that I learned to live sensitively and usefully with the Inuit society. For a period of some years I was called upon to act as a cultural bridge, while always, by my own commitment, working on the growth of Inuit self-sufficiency and self-determination. (At the same time, I was working assiduously as professor and head of the Arctic Research and Training Centre, all paid for by the University of Saskatchewan). It was important to avoid indispensability, as a matter of principle and to gradually withdraw from roles to which the Inuit had greater right, especially as they gained (by experience) competence and confidence.

Animal Versus Human Rights

As the political affairs of the Inuit increasingly engaged the people, I was able to return more fully to observer and consultative roles. But in latter times I found myself drawn again into concern with issues, which once again involved Inuit relationship with nature. This was because of the growing threat to their own identity-giving, life-giving habitat, and their susceptibility yet again to damaging exteriorization. Once again, as in the fur-trade and missionization era, and in the era of government-driven quasi-urbanization—just when they were in the greatest need of identity, solidarity, and cultural health reinforcement (as well as physical health)—exterior forces beyond their control seriously impinged upon their society. I refer to the increasingly embittering results of the campaigns of the animal rights activists that have had direct and harmful impacts on the lives of the Inuit (and indeed on other native people throughout the circumpolar region).

Led initially by Greenpeace, and sustained most notably by a powerful and well-funded organization, an outgrowth of Greenpeace called the International Fund for Animal Welfare, a world-wide campaign of extraordinary virulence has been carried out. It has overtly placed animal rights above human rights, and both indirectly and with increasing frankness displayed raw racism in egregiously distorted statements about the indigenous people and their lives as hunters and trappers. The campaigns began back in the early 1980s in the highly emotional and enormously profitable public attacks on the southern Canadian harp seal hunt, which was augmented by Norwegian participation. The anti-seal hunting campaigns were very successful, not only in stopping Newfoundland and Labrador commercial sealing, but also effectively killing the small market for an entirely different seal product. This was the Arctic-waters ringed seal, taken in a different way by a more remote Aboriginal people who sought essentially to sustain themselves and their relationship with their habitat by the sale of a few pelts not used by themselves for clothing. They hunted mainly ringed and harbour seal, enough for their nutritional and clothing needs in a harsh climate, and, with the small income from the few pelts they sold, were able to outfit themselves for ongoing, self-sustaining intimacy with their traditional habitat. The surplus to domestic-need pelts sold to acquire further hunting supplies rarely exceeded fifteen to twenty per hunter per season, and was usually less.

This hunting is as important for the spiritual and physical welfare of the few regularly employed Inuit as it is for those who depended almost entirely on the sea for sustenance. But the majority of the Inuit have had no regular wage work, and no other form of self-sufficiency. Health, morale, and self-sufficiency in the Arctic radically declined, especially from the early 1980s onwards, after the animal rights campaigns pressed the European Union Parliament into passing legislation banning the importation of North American fur products into the European Union countries. Those countries comprise 70 per cent of the market for Canadian trapping families, the larger proportion of whom are indigenous people who depend on this activity to maintain their practical and spiritual contact with their habitat. Though the full-scale ban was prevented by skilled Inuit and other representations, the already severely damaged market was further harmed by animal rights activists impreciations and distortions, causing increasing trade apprehensions.

For many habitat-oriented Arctic people, the 1980s became a time of despair. Health loss, identity loss, and a sense of futility and helplessness became pervasive. The incidence of suicide, particularly among the young (almost all wage-unemployed but unable now to go out on the land)—became epidemic. Especially among people between fifteen and twenty-five, the rate of self-destruction was 100 per cent higher than elsewhere in Canada, particularly involving males. Drug use and other forms of substance abuse and addiction also became widespread in the mainly young Inuit society. As victims of a formal schooling system which has devalued the traditional culture and those who bear it, and as people seriously bereft of means for self-sufficiency through a relationship with their habitat, the younger Inuit particularly have suffered increasing destitution, social desuetude, and anomie. Only the opportunity for self-renewal through habitat-relatedness offers hope. The loss of the sea-product market, plus the European trapping product ban, seem to have robbed many of the people of that basic hope.

Contemporary Organizational Developments

It is very difficult to maintain a sense of self, either traditional or in the modern socio-economic macro-social context, under such circumstances. I have very briefly described some of the history of disintegration of the collective self, and the loss of context for personal autonomy. It is certainly significant, then, to discover leaders in every Arctic settlement—some young, most middle-aged, many of them women and all respectful of the wisdom of the elderly—still trying to keep their communities and families socially and psychologically viable in the midst of these circumstances. Some leaders are working at regional and national levels, and striving, mainly through the agencies which are successors to earlier parapolitical organizations, to establish a predominantly Inuktitut form of governance in the Canadian Arctic. The new geopolitical unit of Nunavut (Our Land) has emerged as a full participant in the Canadian constitution. The complex social structures of the new administration may possibly offer chances for a new form of Inuktitut self to emerge.

Across the circumpolar reaches in the Inuviaaluit region (around the Beaufort Sea littoral from the MacKenzie Delta area to Holman Island), an Inuit corporate entity has settled its land agreement with Canada, and since 1980 has been developing control over regional affairs. Significantly the Joint Game Council and the process of co-management are at the core of the whole corporate organization. But they too, along with the indigenous people of Arctic Québec and Labrador, Greenland, and Alaska, are curtailed in their economic self-sufficiency by the animal rights campaigns.

A Circumpolar Societal Answer

And yet there may be a circumpolar Inuit answer though barely possible, one which may be applicable in the rest of the world of indigenous people. In 1996 I worked on the European fur ban issue in collaboration with my much more active and involved son, Peter, an Inuk who was at the time in his second year of international lobbying activity for Inuit Tapirisat of Canada, the national representational organization of the Canadian Inuit. It was in England where the extent and emotional momentum of the animal rights campaign seemed overwhelmingly widespread throughout the general population, and therefore espoused earnestly by the election-seeking politicians.

I spent time there speaking as a committed Canadian with the authority of Arctic experience and scholarship as an academic in a variety of centres, with some success. It now transpires that, quite paradoxically, it was Britain which was pressing, in mid-summer of 1997, for the conclusion of the anti-trapping fur-ban issue with a compromise acceptable to the indigenous people. The reason was not really a total change of heart, but fear of World Trade Organization restraint-of-trade sanctions, and desire on the part of the British government to have this troublesome and embarrassing issue off the European agenda before it took its turn with the Union Presidency at the time of the next change. In the end, the human and humane concerns in this issue were resolved in a mode that the indigenous people could accept.

Thus the work has undergone sea-changes since my dog team and iglu-dwelling days. However, the abiding theme of the vital relationship of the autonomous and collective self with the traditional habitat remains. Realizing that this relationship is important to the survival of these living cultural selves, I have begun making an organizational suggestion. There remains much to be researched and implemented concerning other major cultural issues like language, education, and structural factors, but the focus of this discussion has been habitat-relatedness and the integrated self.

The International Indigenous Environmental Agency

I believe that a valuable way of testing the *bona fides* of those who claim primary concern for the world's environment and its creatures is to channel some of the considerable funding spent on these issues into the formation and on-going work of an international indigenous environmental monitoring agency, which would have indigenous leadership guiding the work of Aboriginal people on the ground paid to observe, record, and report on environmental conditions in the habitats to which they have related over millennia of intimacy and respectful stewardship. Thus many would be able to return to their traditional settings—not as Inuit trappers, but as experienced and knowledgeable people doing the various tasks that are necessary to diminish harmful incursions from the world beyond.

Certainly the establishment of such an organization would be inhibited by the bitterness between the animal rights groups and the indigenous people whose lives they have hurt, and that antagonism would have to be overcome. Various indigenous organizations in the world already are organized or developing organizations in this context, but much more extensive and intimate coverage is needed, with the people on the ground and on the sea vitally involved. Thus much more funding is needed. This is where the environmental organizations could be called upon to contribute unconditionally and liberally. Indigenous people and their environment could benefit materially, spiritually, and culturally from their identity-enriching, knowing, and dedicated stewardship. Here is a way in which the indigenous self could be nurtured and re-developed. My ageing self remains whole and well sustained by the two main cultures in my life experience. However, for younger people in the Arctic, both the individuated and collective self is in desperate need of cultural and social sustenance. The opportunity to once again relate realistically to historic habitat is vital to cultural and social survival of indigenous people around the world. The organization I suggest could be a valuable instrument for this broad human purpose.

Nature, Environment, and Community

R. Michael M'Gonigle

JOAN MCINTYRE HAD ASKED TO SPEAK LAST AND SO, WHEN SHE finally took to the podium at week's end, people were tired. "The power is here," she said, looking first at the assembled delegations of the International Whaling Commission (IWC)—and then she reached over to her tape recorder, and pushed PLAY. I had addressed the meeting on the first day when, according to the agenda, the always unwanted non-governmental organizations were given their token turn. I had not understood then why she chose to wait, but now I knew. In that instant, the room was filled with the high, piercing, lyrical crescendo cry of the humpback whale, booming from the speakers, bouncing off the walls. For a whole week, delegates had juggled numbers, repeatedly sent their "scientific advisers" back into closed committees to come up with the right formulas and, in the closing session of this, the IWC's twenty-ninth annual meeting, had finally cut a deal to kill over twenty-three thousand whales over the next year. I had started the meeting excited to have finally joined the small ranks of international whale activists, pleased to be putting in my inaugural week as Greenpeace's first international whale lobbyist. But it was more than I had bargained for—a week of surprises, of shock and growing anger, of deep disillusionment.

And how could I know what was really at stake? I was just a newcomer, a fresh graduate from law school with an interest in international environmental law and a commitment—who knows where from—to help "save the whales." But Joan was different. She had swum with dolphins and whales, had written about them in her counter-cultural classic, *Mind in the Waters* (New York: Charles Scribner's Sons, 1974), and had suffered through many of these annual, control-room, slaughterhouse exercises. As it turned out, this was to be her last IWC meeting, and she wanted to impart a larger message. And in a split second, she did just that, undoing the whole exercise, fracturing the phoney rationality of the assembled delegations, breaking the diplomatic code of cool conduct with the warm, painful, plaintiff call of the humpback whales. The whales, said Joan, were "not represented here." But when they made their entrance, their power was stunning, imposing a full thirty-second moratorium on the deliberations. Only slowly did the delegates begin to recover—to collect their thoughts, adjust themselves in their seats, begin rustling their papers, and reassemble their order.

The year was 1977, and that moment was transformative.

R. MICHAEL M'GONIGLE

A Middle-Class Kid Comes to Love Whales—and Question Authority

Twenty years later, writing this essay, I am forced to ask myself "Why?" Each of us has his own experiences and reasons for embracing environmental values—or not. But why are some, and not others, motivated to take these values further, to make it part of their lives, to take action? And what difference might it make, to you and to the world around you, if you do? These are important questions, not just a matter of personal reflection, at least not if we want to see issues of environmental sustainability move from the periphery of our Western culture to its driving core. It is of course difficult to generalize, but for me there is a clear and simple answer: fishing.

Looking back today, I can see that, like so many others, mine has been a life caught in a dialectical tension that, so unnoticed, nevertheless defines "modern" life. On the one hand is the unreal, but growing, world of the BIG—cities of millions, landscapes of corporate concrete towers, soundscapes of the mass media, lives of plastic consumerism. On the other hand is the real, but disappearing, world of PLACE—neighbourhoods where people live and know each other, small businesses which families actually own, local creeks and woods which await discovery, old stories which our grandparents still tell.

My own story, like those of so many of my generation, has been shaped by this tension. In recollection, it takes off from that day, way back in 1961, when I was young boy in southern Ontario, and my family set out in our Buick Special for the romance and wide open spaces of British Columbia. Growing up in a red-bricked town on the shores of Lake Ontario, I had a typical Canadian upbringing—skating on the roads after a particularly bad winter storm, biking to swim in the local river, fishing from the railway bridge, eating homemade butter tarts on Saturday at the farmers' market on Front Street, gathering at the neighbour's to see the first TV on the block, driving to the edge of town to eat at the first drive-in. But as an over-worked small-town doctor, my father wanted to get away, and took a desk job in Vancouver. We were all lured by visions of the "west beyond the west."

Mine has been a middle-class upbringing and, today, mine is a middle-class life. However unfashionable that may be, it is nonetheless important. For that sector of society is where so many of our environmental problems originate, and it is there too where the power lies to create change.

For my family, the early years didn't work out quite as planned. Never quite able to fit the expectations of a big medical bureaucracy, my father (already in his fifties) soon quit his desk job and found migrant work instead, "doing locums" in a variety of places—in a construction camp for a huge hydroelectric dam in the Rockies near the Alberta border, in a cowtown in the ranch country of the Cariboo, in even smaller logging and fishing villages on northern Vancouver Island. He left the rest of us behind in Vancouver. Our home there was just two houses away from a large stream, Brothers Creek, that ran from Lost Lake near the top of the mountain on Vancouver's North Shore, down to the sea. This was my gang's playground, where we would often start early in the morning and fish our way to the very top of the mountain.

In those years, I was also back and forth between Vancouver and the outposts where my father worked. The activity was always the same—we'd get in the car and go fishing. There was an old ranch that we visited every year in the Cariboo, where we would troll and cast for rainbow trout in the mornings and evenings, and ride horseback through the aspen groves in the afternoons. Once, at a small stream on the coast of Vancouver Island, the water was so low that the salmon couldn't get upstream, and we found ourselves wading in the sea at the river's mouth while the fish, thousands of them, swam around our legs, thrashing in the shallows as they waited for the rain that would let them get upriver. Among them, we felt their fear, and prayed for rain, though I don't remember when it came. Then there was the exotic trip to the Queen Charlotte Islands, home to some of BC's biggest trees, where my father caught his lure on a branch across the river and, rather than break his line, waded across the river to unhook it, water rushing to within an inch of the top of his hipwaders. Lucky he was, and dumb were we both, but he made it back alright. And there were many weekends at home when he and I would just pile into the car, and drive someplace only a couple of hours away but where the trout, salmon, or, best of all, the steelhead were abundant. These were the experiences of many peoples in many places, of fishers and ranchers, miners and chokermen, Indians old and young, in small places in a wild country, all then newfound friends of my father.

For most of this time we lived on Vancouver's North Shore, looking up the hill at the sprawling houses in the "British Properties," houses that were climbing ever further up the mountain, deeper and deeper into the forest. For whatever reasons—maybe it was the contrast between East and West, city and country, comfortable suburb and my father off somewhere trying to make a living—I developed an ambivalence in those years that I was not really to understand until much later. But the stimulus was everywhere. My creek, for example, was largely a wild place when I got there. We drank from it all the time, and it was full of trout. But as one house after another popped up right beside the creekbed, I felt the impacts as the banks slid down and the septic tanks spilled into the water. By the time I graduated from high school, my creek was virtually dead—channelized, culverted, polluted. None of us understood why they had to build so close. Even then, people talked about the "nature strips" that somebody said they had in Australia.

And then there was the incident with the trees. The main road down below us was being upgraded to a four-lane highway and, in the process, the contractors decided to take down some very large trees. They were nowhere near the right-of-way, but were close to the creek, so the alarm went out. Everyone rallied, parents and all. We went to the forest, and got right in there, surrounding the trees, stopping the chainsaws. In an act unnoticed and now all but forgotten, my whole neighbourhood engaged in one of the world's early examples of tree hugging. To everyone's surprise, the Highways official agreed with us and told us not to worry, the trees could stay. So we all went home, smiling with victory. The next day, after school and after work, we came home to find that all the trees were gone.

In those years, we drove on a lot of logging roads in search of the best fishing spots, and everywhere we went there were clear-cuts right down to the river's edge. Like my own local stream, it made no sense to either of us. On one trip in the mid 1960s, we went fishing for salmon off northern Vancouver Island. As we puttered along in our small rented boat, we spotted a large ship on the horizon coming toward us. As it approached, we could see that it was an unusual vessel, and that it was towing something very big. Soon we found ourselves face to face with a whaling ship coming home. It was towing a large cluster of sperm whales, recently killed in the North Pacific. To both of us, the sight was so profoundly disturbing that we gave up our own quest at harvesting the bounty of the local inlet, and put in to the dock at Coal Harbour—right next to the flensing deck of the last whaling station on Canada's west coast. By this time, the whales were being hauled up. One at a time, a heavy hook was sunk into each whale's flesh and, as it was pulled in, several people sliced away on each side, winching off long fat strips of whale meat from the bloody and fast-diminishing carcass. The sound of pulling, tearing, and ripping was more than either of us could bear. We left quickly, but the memory, and the sounds, linger still.

Neither a street kid nor the victim of an abusive family, my formative experiences and youthful middle-class struggles were less dramatic, but no less important. Like so many Canadians then and now, mine were the unselfconscious experiences of community and territory—experienced, threatened, and often lost. And for what?

From Creek to Conference Hall—and Back

If my experience at Coal Harbour didn't drive me into law school, it certainly gave me the direction to do what I did when I got there, and to resist the omnipresent pressure of the big firm. The forces guiding me were still too subtle for me to know just why. I knew that I wanted to work in international environmental law, and yet I spent my summers while at university working as a labourer on pipeline projects and hydroelectric dams, with scarcely a thought for the consequences. After all, that's what every student did during the summer in BC back then. (More recently, the standard job has been tree-planting.) But it hit me, I remember, in 1972. Two high school buddies and I drove from town to town that summer in an old Volkswagen Beetle looking for yet another pipeline job, all the while following the comings and goings of the first UN Conference on the Human Environment in Stockholm. The contrast, and the choice, was apparent.

A few years later, with my law school credentials in hand, I had my opportunity. After much pacing back and forth in my apartment, I finally got up the nerve to take the plunge, and arranged a meeting with the fledgling Vancouver group, Greenpeace. It was so easy in those days: I walked down the street to the small corner office, met the people familiar from the newspaper pictures—Bob Hunter, Paul Spong, and Pat Moore—and made them an offer. A year earlier, in 1975, Greenpeace had grabbed the world's headlines with its footage of the Russian whaler harpooning a whale over Greenpeace's camera-equipped protest boats on the high seas. But the power to stop this carnage was elsewhere, I argued; it was in the distant corridors of international diplomacy. They agreed and, right away, I was set loose. Get Greenpeace accredited to the IWC, and get whaling banned!

And so, for the next several years, I wandered the corridors of power, travelling from one international meeting to another, drafting position papers for the conference hall, and holding up banners for the street rallies and the press. Through quota debates and partial moratoriums, I experienced the to-and-fro-ing of high politics and high places. It was an exhilarating journey. For one thing, in those years Greenpeace was growing everywhere. By the end of the decade, I found myself living in Washington, DC, our battle to create an international organization out of Greenpeace won, and the new head office of Greenpeace International just down the street from my apartment.

The place, and the time too, was exhilarating, but it didn't last as the ambivalence between BIG and PLACE began to set in. When I had first met Joan McIntyre a few years earlier in Canberra, I was of course all pumped about what I was doing, and where I was doing it. Joan had a different take on the burgeoning environmental jet set.

"You're too much Greenpeace," she told me, "and not enough whales." I was hurt at her having pricked my personal, fast-inflating balloon, but I could also see what she was getting at. In Washington, her words came back to haunt me. There, you could talk whales all month, and never see one, and never even smell the salt air for years on end.

At the time, I was also completing graduate work on the east coast and, through it, becoming more and more aware of the nature of the contradiction which imbues the soul of Washington—the contradiction of a structure of wealth and power that comes from who-knows-where, the contradiction of a growth machine that keeps the system going while it erodes the very base on which its future depends. For me, the straw that broke my back was the passage of an energy bill supported by that quintessential, well-intentioned liberal, Jimmy Carter. The bill allocated some $3 billion to renewable energy—and $88 billion to extracting synthetic fuel oil from coal. As Carter fell to Reagan, the abstraction of it all, the contradictions of the solutions being offered, and my own ambivalence took me over. In a way, I understood the neoconservative onslaught that soon stormed the American capital. "Which way is it going to be?" I kept asking. One has to choose.

And there was another gnawing pressure too. The summer before we left Washington, my wife—Wendy Wickwire—and I were in BC. She was doing fieldwork with First Nations elders, and I was working on my thesis. Car-camping on the west side of the Fraser River, we picked a spot by a smaller river that flowed into the Fraser, and set up our tent for a few days. While she travelled around interviewing Native elders, I stayed put to read, and fish. As usual, it took me a while to notice but, after several days, I finally realized that there was no road along this river, just a foot trail up through the canyon. We asked the Forest Service officer tending our campsite about this unknown valley. He shook his head in dismay, telling us of the roadbuilding and logging plans, and of a small lobby group, just a handful of people, working to stop them.

On that first visit to the Stein River, we walked upstream with some local children from the Indian reserve, and watched them fish their favourite pools. We had picnics on the bluff by the sidecreeks flowing into the Stein, and wondered what was depicted on the faded rock paintings above us. We feasted on ripe saskatoon berries and, best of all, drank the cold clear water that rushed down from the snowpack high above us. And then, as we were leaving, one of those things happened that, well, you just don't usually talk about, let alone write about, because it sounds just too hokey and far-fetched. Nevertheless, as we drove along the dirt road, we stopped for a last look up the valley before turning the corner that would take it out of our view, and start us back on our journey home. It had been raining earlier, but had now stopped, so we got out of the car and leaned against a fence post. "What are we going to do?" I asked. There was, of course, no answer really, as we were soon heading back to Washington. But at that moment, arcing over the valley where the mountains tighten right in on the river, a rainbow appeared. Right there.

And so we came back to BC the next fall, late in 1982, the year our burgeoning conservation movement achieved a global moratorium on commercial whaling. We left our apartment in DC and rented a cabin by the Stein River, on the outskirts of the town of Lytton. This was a world different from any that either of us had lived in, but to me, the place was home, and it was familiar. And it was, well, on the ground. To get to our cabin, you had to cross the Fraser by an unmotorized, two-car "reaction ferry" that is propelled by the current of that mighty river. We both now had PhDs in hand, but were soon getting by on $10,000 a year. Instead of flying to London with my urbane environmental colleagues, I now found myself hiking in the alpine with a gaggle of elementary school kids from the local town and the reserve. Instead of organizing press conferences in hotel suites in Tokyo, I was setting up a wilderness program in the cluttered offices of the manager of the Mount Currie Indian Band.

But there was something else too, as we recollected in the book that Wendy and I wrote as part of the wilderness campaign, *Stein: The Way of the River* (Vancouver: Talonbooks, 1988). Here, in this valley we had happened upon

> *a rare surviving microcosm of both nature and history—of grizzly bear and Native shaman, of old trapper and clear running river.*
>
> *How can one convey the meaning of wilderness—the purpose and value of a wild thicket, remote from the everyday world, accessible only on foot and with patience? To a society perpetually rushing to the next appointment, wilderness is an antidote for our self-absorption. In wilderness is perfection without self-consciousness, a rich complexity of life woven into a dynamic wholeness that pulsates with vitality, yet is quiet to behold. In the flow and dance of a running stream is the movement of life itself.*

It was here, I think, in my years at the Stein, that the point of my own education really—how can I say it?—came together. On the one hand, at that place, Wendy and I discovered something infinitely valuable and precious, and yet so clearly threatened and, in fact, inevitably dying. The Stein may never be logged, but now, fifteen years later, the elders that we spent time with are all dead. Here, as elsewhere in the world, with their deaths, the language of local peoples is being silenced to a whisper, and is about to disappear entirely. Here, as elsewhere, the experiences of local places, when there is yet wild spaces and spirits in those spaces, is eroding away. Here, as elsewhere, the strength and diversity and skills of a community living long with its place, and functioning together, is becoming but a romantic memory. In British Columbia, industrial forestry cuts over 70 million cubic metres of old-growth forest every year, and its devastating march continues unabated. The five-year "development plan" drives all, as the short-term conquest drives out the long-term balance. In the process, the relentless quest for corporate profit snuffs out the age-old embodiment of cultural value. Thus does the BIG consume the PLACE.

What I Learned from the Banners, and the Books

One of the advantages of spending time around the university is that occasionally living pieces of history come to visit. When I was an undergraduate at the University of British Columbia in the 1960s, Alexander Kerensky, the head of the provisional government in Russia in 1917 after the Tsar and before the Bolsheviks, actually came to speak. I thought of that event a few years ago when I saw a small poster advertising a talk by one of the radical old greats of postwar economic thinking, Andre Gunter Frank. This was a name from the 1960s, like Herbert Marcuse. He's still kicking, I thought, and still has something to say.

Many others on the campus were equally excited and, on the day of Frank's talk, the conference room at the Halpern Centre at Simon Fraser University was packed. When I arrived, the many aisles of chairs were already filled, and all around people were sitting on the floor and leaning against the wall. Professor Frank was at the front, fresh off the plane from his home in Amsterdam. Frank is famous for his pathbreaking critique of the 1950s myths of international development. At a time when everyone else was mapping out the "stages of economic growth" for the newly decolonized countries, he coined the phrase "the development of underdevelopment" to describe what he saw as an opposing process, a new form of perpetual colonialism driven by the inequities of economic growth. His so-called "dependency theory" has since become a staple of Left politics.

But the eager anticipation of Frank's talk quickly gave way to gasps of disbelief. As he spoke, he again assaulted conventional wisdom, not by recanting his socialism, but by rejecting history itself. In essence, he said that it's all basically the same—capitalism, socialism, communism. Marginal differences exist, but for five thousand years it's been conquest and growth, for the benefit of a few. The general target of his attack was clear—the West, centralized power, even civilization itself. Whether it was Ramses II or Rockefeller III, our history can be seen as a constant drive for central power, at the expense of "the people," a common characteristic of corporate capitalism and state socialism alike. Needless to say, these sweeping historical heresies did not go down well with an academic audience, especially with the many Marxists and historians in the crowd where the outrage was palpable.

Frank's heresy left me feeling uneasy—but excited. Many disagreed with the way he collapsed distinctions, but his basic point was deeply liberating. After all, if capitalism and socialism, while important, weren't the real parameters of history, what might a larger dynamic entail? And, although Frank didn't explain this for me, my own experiences did, pointing me to an understanding of a new "ecological political economy." Unlike prevalent theories of political economy—from liberal to Marxist—an ecological political economy brings physical relations (in a variety of manifestations) into the social world, and *vice versa*. From this perspective, my own experience of BIG vs. PLACE can be seen from the even larger vantage point of two opposing tendencies—or, to put it another way, two idealized forms of social organization—that exist as a dynamic tension, or dialectic, in all human relations and societies.

In my own work, today, I call these tendencies "centre" and "territory," tendencies which are applicable to the whole range of human cultural experience. Centre is manifest in hierarchical organizations built around the imperatives of concentrated power and bigness. Centrist structures are necessarily sustained by resources and flows of energy from somewhere else. In contrast, territorial forms of social organization are rooted in forms of social power which are dispersed and on-the-ground, and can be maintained by local resources. While centre and territory have a physical or geographic component to them, they are not just that, but are also omnipresent tendencies in social organization and cultural consciousness that intermingle in various degrees and manifestations in the things and acts of everyday life. Centre is, for example, manifest in the processes at the IWC and the new houses creeping up the mountain. But territory is manifest in the

neighbours who, while they live in these new houses, also get together to protect the forest that survives.

When one re-examines the past and present of evolution of Western societies, a basic contradiction in these forces appears. In short, the rise of central power is, and always has been, sustained by the territorial structures that precede that rise, and it cannot survive without them. Yet, driven to grow, centralist institutions consume the very territorial processes on which they depend. In doing so, they await their own demise. This is the story of countless civilizations past that have risen, only to fall. And today, this is the character of the centre-driven, entropy-creating consumer society spreading out into every forest and every fishing creek on the globe. Thus do territorial forms permeate the big city, while centrism pervades even the most remote places. And, like the shapes of our own lives, these forces pull and push us in many, often contradictory, directions.

In this situation, the significance of the tension between centre and territory is in the dialectic itself. It lies in the tension between linear and circular processes of life. To understand the dynamics of these modes of organizing power is the task of an ecological political economy. How have the universal tendencies to centre power been held in check by territorial institutions, and how might they again? How might centralist institutions in the future be reconfigured to enforce, rather than erode, territorialist values at all levels? Organizing the world to maintain the continuous flow of resources to, and up, these hierarchies is what the modern project has been all about. To challenge the modern world system with its centralized hierarchies of power that are sustained by nonlocal resources is the task of a territorialist environmentalism. All our efforts at saving and protecting are part of the far larger struggle to maintain, and strengthen, territorial forces of equity and community, diversity, and ecology that provide the essential counter-balance to centrist power and hierarchical growth.

Nature, Environment . . . and Community

A couple of years ago, over a hundred activists gathered at the First Nations Longhouse on the grounds of the University of British Columbia. The premier of the province, Mike Harcourt, stepped to the microphone to announce a new provincial park for the Stein Valley. Everyone who had worked on this campaign over the past twenty plus years was excited, and relieved. Finally, perhaps, that struggle was over. And yet many recognized that it wasn't. This premier had created over one hundred new parks in his term of office, a huge achievement, but the niggling concern would not go away. Parks or not, nothing had really changed with the forest industry that was still gnawing away around the edges.

As I write this, a second-term government is in power, still a social democratic government, and the news is not good. The new premier of British Columbia, Glen Clark, is a former labour organizer, and has little time for environmentalists who might threaten that linear flow of resources on which capital, and labour, and government, indeed, on which we all, depend. And so when Greenpeace recently exposed the failures in the government's forest practices regulations, and threatened an international campaign against the industry, the premier decried the organization as "enemies of the people." More recently, the head of the woodworkers union publicly complained that there were "too many goddamned parks," and that logging should start inside them.

Meanwhile, Japan and Norway, using a loophole in the regulations, are still whaling, and threatening to leave the IWC unless commercial whaling is permitted again. Despite the victories of my own short contribution to the environmental movement, nothing I have experienced and worked for is yet safe. New rules are on the statute books, and many how-to books are in the library. But everywhere the creeks are still dying, the forests are still falling, and the communities of place are still being pushed aside and pushed under. As a culture, we have not yet begun to live in and with our places, and until we do that, we cannot know what we are losing.

Play it again, Joan!

Century of the Environment

Edward O. Wilson

BECAUSE I'M SO OFTEN IDENTIFIED IN THE MEDIA AS THE "ANT man," I thought it would be appropriate to make several comments about these wonderful little insects. There are about one thousand trillion ants in the world alive at any given moment, and all together they weigh about as much as all of human beings combined. They turn more soil than earthworms, catch more harmful insects than birds, and serve as the cemetery squads to remove more than 90 per cent of dead insects and other small animals . . . so we don't have to worry about going around and picking up these icky things ourselves. And ants, with their exquisite colony organization, show us that socialism works! Yes, Karl Marx, in spite of what you've been taught, was right! He just had the wrong creatures. He should have been an entomologist, and studied ants at Harvard. These are among the reasons for my answer to the most common question I'm asked about ants. People say, what should I do about the ants in my kitchen? And I say, watch where you step! Be careful of little lives. Put out some cookie crumbs; ants also like honey and sugar water. Get down and watch them closely, and you will see a remarkable social existence so different from our own that they might have come from a different planet. We don't have to go to Mars or even watch *Independence Day* on video to see something utterly alien.

The achievements of ants are enormous. When President Lowell gave an honorary degree to the great ant expert William Morton Wheeler in the 1920s, he read this encomium: "Professor Wheeler has shown us that ants, like human beings, can create civilizations without the use of reason." And that brings us to the dark side of what I like to call these little things that run the world. They are the most warlike of all organisms, much more so than human beings. Colonies repeatedly attack other colonies and wipe them out if they can. Ants commit genocide routinely. If they had nuclear weapons, they would wipe out the world in a week. King Solomon was wrong when he said, "Go to the ants thou sluggard, and be wise." Max Beerbohm, the humorist, was right when he wrote in his famous notebook, "The ant has a lesson to teach us all, and it is not good."

But . . . to look down to earth, to the soil, and the myriad little creatures on whose lives our lives depend, is to bear in mind that the environment matters, and crucially. We must never forget what sustains us on this planet. All human beings want three things for themselves and their families: health, a meaningful existence, and a pleasant environment. The big news of our time is that all three are locked together, and will become more so with the passage of each year. Our health, our livelihood, our very perception of the fulfillment of life depends on how we protect and manage the environment.

Still, we are doing a wretched job at protecting and managing the environment, in spite of all the talk about it. In 1946, when I started college, there were 2 billion people on Earth. Now there are 6 billion; in thirty years there will be 8 billion. The sheer weight of humanity is more than a hundred times greater than any large animal that ever lived on the land. Our species *Homo sapiens*, although only one out of more than 10 million species on Earth, appropriates an incredible 40 per cent of the energy fixed by green plants on the land as particulate matter. And we should pay attention to the fact that the poor people of the world are gaining a larger and larger share of the world population. In 1946 two-thirds of humanity lived in the developing countries. Today it is four-fifths, in thirty years it will be five-sixths. Almost one billion of these people, the bottom billion they are called, live in what the United Nations classifies as absolute poverty, struggling to survive from one day to the next, often going hungry. A half million children die each year from starvation or starvation-related diseases. These people are not on another planet. They are in increasingly close touch with us, their problems are becoming our problems, their wars our wars, their inability to function and produce our lost markets.

These poor of the Earth are destroying their own environment. The rain forests, which hold the richest faunas and floras in the world—literally a majority of all the species—the rain forests that potentially could be so highly productive economically for all the world, are being cut and burned and turned into wastelands at the rate of as much as 1 per cent of their cover each year—70,000 square kilometres, an area half that of the state of Florida. In thirty years a third or more of that forest will be gone and with it 20 per cent of all the species living there lost forever. Used wisely, however, these environments and others in similar danger, the grasslands, lakes, rivers, and coral reefs, cannot only be saved but turned into sources of new products, new crops, new pharmaceuticals, new petroleum substitutes, on a sustained-yield basis. The developing countries can create natural products far beyond the capability of the industrialized nations; this is an important way for them to gain economic parity and strength as trading partners.

That is in part why, on a global basis, we can be said to have entered the Century of the Environment, and this is where young people come in. We are embarked on an age when we must—and we will—put our house in order in North America but also assist the developing world, where the bulk of humanity lives, to seek affluence while preserving its vast natural heritage.

To say that we have entered the Century of the Environment is also to recognize the fact that we are coming to depend more intensely on developments in science and technology. Medicine, I'm sure you're aware, has turned increasingly into an exercise in genetics and molecular biology. Biologists have discovered a genetic basis for colon cancer, for a propensity to Alzheimer's disease and heart disease, even for a tendency to schizophrenia and alcoholism. Malfunctions from cancer to kidney failure are thought of now in terms of metabolic pathways and magic bullets that restore and heal. The common phrase you hear in the laboratory is: all disease is genetic.

To an increasing degree even moral reasoning turns upon scientific knowledge of life's great problems. Witness the abortion controversy, cloning, the joint issue of crime and drug abuse, regulation of the tobacco industry, the questions of acid rain and greenhouse warming of the climate, and, not least, international terrorism. It is a remarkable fact that half the legislation coming before Congress at the present time is to some extent guided by a knowledge of science and technology.

The trend is very clear: involvement in science and technology will be increasingly environment-oriented. Whether to allow a landfill to proceed, whether to insist on industrial scrubbers, whether to push for a natural reserve instead of a housing development are just the beginning issues, the surface issues. Overfishing in international waters, foreign aid for environmental improvement instead of military armament, the promotion of population control are among the larger, politico-environmental issues that will determine the fate of the world.

There are two major categories of environmental problems, and only two: degradation of the physical environment and loss of biological diversity. Environmental degradation can be reversed; such billion-dollar steps as cleaning up Boston Harbor are necessary, expensive, and, let me emphasize, relatively boring. Stopping the loss of biological diversity by slowing species extinction is, in sharp contrast, irreversible. It is not boring, and it can be immensely profitable. The species of plants and animals going extinct by the thousands each year in North America and abroad in places like the Amazon rain forest are the potential source of wealth and security for the whole world. Whether they continue to live or die will have a profound effect on the stability of the ecosystems, and the quality of the environment in which we live.

So let us use science to the maximum, as a way of thinking and as a manual for the making of wise decisions in the increasingly complicated but hopeful future of the new century. And always, without fail, let us all be environmentalists, in order to avoid the ignorant mistakes of previous generations, keeping in mind that we are a part of the Creation—the living world—in body and spirit. We belong on this planet as a biological heritage, and we have a sacred personal duty to keep it intact and healthy.

On behalf of my friends, the ants and other little creatures teeming at your feet, please be careful. I am serious: they are more important than you might have guessed.

The Contributors

MICHAEL ALEKSIUK spent the 1950s roaming the then-pristine boreal forests in northern Alberta, observing and reflecting on nature. He earned his PhD in zoology at the University of British Columbia, taught human biology, and published some forty research papers as a tenured professor at the University of Manitoba. He then spent several years conducting environmental research and studying human behaviour in the industrial sector. In 1986 he left industry to become an independent scholar and writer. He wrote a weekly newspaper column titled "Nature, Environment and People," and published a book of human behaviour titled *Power Therapy*. In 1996 Michael accepted an invitation to work with Professor Thomas Nelson in the Department of Psychology at the University of Alberta, where he spent five years as a senior research associate. Alas, Michael found academia stifling to his creativity, and has once again chosen to become an independent scholar and writer.

MICHAEL ALEKSIUK, WINDSOR PARK PLAZA, 409–11135–83 AVENUE, EDMONTON, AB, CANADA T6G 2C6

CHERYL LOUSLEY comes from a small hamlet in eastern Ontario called Bishops Mills. She currently resides in Toronto where she is pursuing a PhD in environmental literature and cultural studies at York University, and is active with several local environmental, cycling, and social justice groups. She dedicates this piece to her longtime walking and cross-country skiing companion—her family's border collie, Belle, who passed away in April 2001.

CHERYL LOUSLEY, FACULTY OF ENVIRONMENTAL STUDIES, YORK UNIVERISTY, TORONTO, ON, CANADA M3P 1J3

LISA LYNCH earned her master's degree in eco-psychology, and is currently serving as Chair of Integrative Studies in Psychology at Antioch University, Seattle. She is currently pursuing her PhD in eco-psychology at the Union Institute. Lisa has also been in training to become a wilderness vision fast guide with the School of Lost Borders and takes groups out for weekend and week-long wilderness rites-of-passage quests.

LISA M. LYNCH, 1026 GLEN STREET, EDMONDS, WA, USA 98020

R. MICHAEL M'GONIGLE holds the Eco-Research Chair of Environmental Law and Policy at the University of Victoria. A lawyer and political economist, he also directs POLIS, a newly created think tank on ecological governance. A graduate of the London School of Economics and Yale University, he is a lifelong activist and co-founded Greenpeace International, the Sierra Legal Defense Fund, and, most recently, Smart Growth BC, Forest Futures, and the International Network of Forests and Communities.

R. MICHAEL M'GONIGLE, ECO-RESEARCH CHAIR OF ENVIRONMENTAL LAW & POLICY, FACULTY OF LAW & SCHOOL OF ENVIRONMENTAL STUDIES, UNIVERSITY OF VICTORIA, VICTORIA, BC, CANADA V8W 3H7

TOM NELSON began his formal working life as a teenaged soldier in war-torn Europe. He entered university upon his return, eventually earning his doctorate in psychology at Michigan State University. Following a six-year period dedicated to research, Tom accepted a position as associate professor of psychology at the University of Alberta in 1964. He served as professor and chair of the Department from 1967 to 1985. Tom has published over 120 papers in journals and books, and, currently retired as University (Distinguished) Professor at U of A, continues to publish in peer-reviewed journals. But Tom is more than an academic: he is very much a man of the land. Early on, he and his wife reforested an abandoned farm where the soil had become nutrient-depleted. He is currently in the process of restoring an abandoned homestead north of Athabasca.

THOMAS MORGAN NELSON, DEPARTMENT OF PSYCHOLOGY, UNIVERSITY OF ALBERTA, EDMONTON, AB, CANADA T6G 2E9

At the time of writing his essay, RICHARD PICKARD was completing a doctorate on eighteenth-century English poetry and working on contract for the British Columbia Ministry of Environment, Lands and Parks. He received his PhD from the University of Alberta in 1998.

Currently he is a senior policy analyst for the BC Pension Corporation, and an occasional writer.

RICHARD PICKARD, RICHARDPICKARD@YAHOO.COM

Born in York, England, DOUG PORTEOUS began work as a postman at age eight, graduating to shop assistant, shipyard labourer, and factory worker. He enjoyed an education at Oxford (BA, MA), Hull (PhD), Harvard and MIT (postdoctoral), and has also relished being a hitchhiker, volcano-climber, pilgrim, poet, glider pilot, tour guide, and Arctic kayaker. He teaches geography at the University of Victoria, British Columbia, has written twelve books, travels globally, and landscapes gardens locally.

J. DOUGLAS PORTEOUS, DEPARTMENT OF GEOGRAPHY, UNIVERSITY OF VICTORIA, P.O. BOX 3050 VICTORIA, BC, CANADA V8W 3P5

MARK SCHALLER was born into a family that moved often. He spent chunks of his childhood in India, Pakistan, and Tanzania, as well the eastern United States. Since then, he's lived amid the big landscapes of the west. After getting a PhD in psychology from Arizona State University, Mark taught at universities in Texas and Montana. He's now at the University of British Columbia, in Vancouver, where he lives near the water and escapes into the mountains.

MARK SCHALLER, DEPARTMENT OF PSYCHOLOGY, UNIVERSITY OF BRITISH COLUMBIA, 2136 WEST MALL, VANCOUVER, BC, CANADA V6T 1Z4

MAURICE STRONG was born and raised in Manitoba, Canada. He led the United Nations Conference on the Human Environment held in Stockholm in 1972, became the first executive director of the newly formed UN Environment Programme in 1973, and served as the secretary-general of the 1992 UN Conference on Environment and Development in Rio. He led UN Secretary-General Annan's program of reforming the United Nations for the purpose of making it a more workable organization. Although an extraordinarily busy man, he still visits relatives in Edmonton and Winnipeg at every opportunity.

MAURICE STRONG, CHAIRMAN, EARTH COUNCIL, 401–255 CONSUMERS ROAD, NORTH YORK, ON, CANADA M2J 5B6

IAIN TAYLOR is a botanist, science ethicist, and professor at the University of British Columbia Botanical Garden. He earned degrees from the University of Liverpool, taught high school, and worked at the University of Texas before coming to Canada. He is a founding member of the Association of Professional Biologists of British Columbia and a former president of the Canadian Botanical Association. He spends his summers converting a wilderness farm into a native flower garden.

IAIN E. P. TAYLOR, BOTANICAL GARDEN AND DEPARTMENT OF BOTANY, UNIVERSITY OF BRITISH COLUMBIA, 6804 SOUTHWEST MARINE DRIVE, VANCOUVER, BC, CANADA V6T 1Z4

ARITHA VAN HERK is a hiker, reader, and writer, who has had various encounters with landscape and nature in her novels, *Judith, The Tent Peg, No Fixed Address*, and *Places Far From Ellesmere*. Her books of ficto-criticism, *In Visible Ink* and *A Frozen Tongue*, are concerned with articulating the inarticulable. *Restlessness*, her fifth work, is a fictional manual on how to evade travel and avoid story while stopped at the crossroads of death and homesickness. *Mavericks: An Incorrigible History of Alberta* appeared in 2001. She teaches Canadian literature and creative writing at the University of Calgary.

ARITHA VAN HERK, DEPARTMENT OF ENGLISH, UNIVERSITY OF CALGARY, CALGARY, AB, CANADA T2N 1N4

ROBERT WILLIAMSON, PhD, professor of anthropology emeritus at the University of Saskatchewan, conducted research in the Canadian Arctic for forty-two years, twenty-two of which were spent travelling and living on the land—summer and winter—with contemporary Inuit society. He is fluent in Inuktitut, the Inuit language. Robert prefers dog-team travelling and iglu life with Inuit to snowmobile roaring and modern winter-tent sojourning, wishing to see and hear the environment better. Robert founded the magazine *Inuktitut*, and was the initiator of the Arctic Research and Training Centre at Rankin Inlet, NWT, where he served as head. He was the first Inuktitut-speaking person to be elected to the NWT Legislative Council. Currently a research associate in the Arctic Institute of North America and an adjunct professor of both anthropology and communication and culture at the University of Calgary, Dr. Williamson remains active in advocacy on Arctic human ecological matters. He became a member of the Order of Canada in 1985.

ROBERT G. WILLIAMSON, ARCTIC INSTITUTE OF NORTH AMERICA, UNIVERSITY OF CALGARY, AB, CANADA T2N 1N4

E. O. WILSON, Pellegrino University Professor Emeritus at Harvard, is considered by many to be the single most insightful scholar of the late twentieth century. A prolific writer and winner of two Pulitzer Prizes, *On Human Nature* (1978) and *The Ants* (1990), with Bert Hölldobler, he is best known among academics for his groundbreaking treatise *Sociobiology: The New Synthesis*. That book triggered a paradigm shift that set psychology on a solid biological foundation. Wilson's book *Consilience: The Unity of Knowledge*, published in 1998, has implications for most fields of scholarly endeavour.

EDWARD O. WILSON, MUSEUM OF COMPARATIVE ZOOLOGY, HARVARD UNIVERSITY, 26 OXFORD STREET, CAMBRIDGE, MA 02138-2902.

Acknowledgements

The editors thank Drs. Gene Lechelt, Gay Bisanz, and Charles Beck of the Department of Psychology at the University of Alberta for their moral and material support during the conceptualization, planning, and completion of this book project. Isaac Lank of that department provided computer support, and Chris Boyle typed portions of the manuscript. This project was financed in part by a grant from the Alberta Foundation for the Arts to senior editor Michael Aleksiuk. Don Kerr, professor of English at the University of Saskatchewan and press editor at NeWest Press, provided invaluable input at the final editing stage of the project. Last but not least, the editors thank the authors of individual chapters for responding to editorial suggestions graciously, expertly, and promptly.

NEW LEAF PAPER

ENVIRONMENTAL BENEFITS STATEMENT

Landscapes of the Heart is printed on New Leaf EcoBook, made with 100% post-consumer waste, processed chlorine free. By using this environmentally friendly paper, NeWest Press saved the following resources:

trees	water	electricity	solid waste	greenhouse gases
13 fully grown	1,256 gallons	1,638 kilowatt hours	3 cubic yards	2,075 pounds

Calculated based on research done by the Environmental Defense and other members of the Paper Task Force.

 Visit us in cyberspace at www.newleafpaper.com or call 1-888-989-5323

NEW LEAF
PAPER